Days of the Rebels

Above: *By 1838 the British garrison in the Canadas numbered 8,000 men. These Grenadier Guards were brought from England to suppress the rebellions of 1837.*

Previous page: *Thomas Conant's grandfather was one casualty of the days of the rebels — killed outside his home by a drunken dispatch rider. But in the eyes of the law he was a rebel, and during the trial, testimony of witnesses was not admitted. In the chaos of political violence many personal feuds were settled.*

1822

Canadian Trade Act, regulating commercial and financial relations of Upper and Lower Canada, passed in British Parliament.

1823

Canadian Magazine published in Montreal.

John Rowand establishes HBC Northwest headquarters at Edmonton House.

John Caldwell is dismissed as receiver-general of L.C. for defrauding government of £96,000.

1824

William Lyon Mackenzie establishes the *Colonial Advocate* in Queenston, U.C.

COLONIAL ADVOCATE.

Reformers gain majority in elections for U.C. Assembly.

First road cut from Edmonton House to Fort Assiniboine.

Lachine Canal is completed.

Literary and Historical Society of Quebec founded.

The *Canadian Review* published in Montreal.

Controversy rages over equal status of the Church of England and the Scottish Kirk in U.C.

Julia Hart publishes *Saint Ursula's Convent or The Nun of Canada,* the first English language Canadian novel.

1825

Fort Vancouver is founded as Pacific headquarters for the HBC.

Fire destroys Miramichi, N.B.

Halifax Banking Company established.

BANK.

THE Subscribers respectfully acquaint the public, that they have entered into copartnership for the establishment of a BANK, under the firm of "The HALIFAX BANKING COMPANY." They have appropriated a large capital exclusively to this object, and have opened their Bank for Business, in the new Stone Building owned by Mr. Collins. The Company are fully sensible that the success of the Institution must depend upon the friendly support which it may receive from the Community, and earnestly solicit the public patronage in its behalf.

HENRY COGSWELL, President.
WILLIAM PRYOR, Vice President.
ENOS COLLINS
JAMES TOBIN,
SAMUEL CUNARD,
JOHN CLARK,
JOSEPH ALLISON
MARTIN GAY BLACK,

N. B. Hours for business from 10 to 3 o'clock, every day; Sundays and Holidays at the Public offices, excepted.
Discount days, Tuesdays and Thursdays.
Halifax, August 31, 1825.

Oliver Goldsmith publishes *The Rising Village,* the first book of poems by a native English-Canadian.

David Willson builds the Temple of Sharon for the "Children of Peace" sect in U.C.

The Erie Canal completed between Albany and Buffalo, New York, threatening St. Lawrence commerce.

Anglo-Russian Treaty fixes boundary of Alaska at 54°40′.

1826

La Minerve published in Montreal.

Bytown (Ottawa) founded by Colonel John By.

John Galt's Canada Company purchases 1,100,000 acres of Crown Reserves land known as The Huron Tract.

Egerton Ryerson publishes an attack on Anglican Archdeacon John Strachan, beginning their lifelong feud.

Family Compact scions destroy the offices of the *Colonial Advocate* and toss W. L. Mackenzie's press into the Don River.

STATEMENT OF FACTS,

RELATING TO THE TRESPASS

ON THE

PRINTING PRESS,

IN THE POSSESSION OF MR. WILLIAM LYON MACKENZIE,

IN JUNE, 1826.

ADDRESSED TO THE PUBLIC GENERALLY.

AND

PARTICULARLY TO THE SUBSCRIBERS AND SUPPORTERS

OF THE

COLONIAL ADVOCATE.

ANCASTER:

PRINTED BY GEO. GURNETT.

1828.

General Mining Association formed to begin exploitation of N.S. coal.

1827

British Parliament authorizes the sale of Clergy Reserve lands.

SALE OF CROWN LANDS.

THE undermentioned CROWN LANDS, in the Districts and Counties below mentioned, (being Lots specially applied for to purchase,) will be offered for sale, by auction, IN THE MONTH OF NOVEMBER next, upon the usual terms and conditions.

For times and places of sale, reference is requested to the General Notice from this Office for Crown Lands and Clergy Reserves, of the 7th June ultimo.

WESTERN DISTRICT.
County of Kent.
SOMBRA.

2nd Con. Lot B. 30 acres, fronts on River St. Clair.
Do. do. N. part 26, 30 acres, north side of Bear Creek.
Do. do. N. part 27, 30 do. do. do. do.
3rd do. Lot B. 10 acres, fronts on the River St. Clair.
Do. do. E. part N. half 11, 40 acres, fronts on Bear Creek.

Fort Langley on the Fraser River settled by Lt. Aemilius Simpson and HBC Chief Trader, James McMillan.

Joseph Howe purchases the *Nova-scotian.*

Sir John Colbourne appointed lieutenant-governor of U.C.

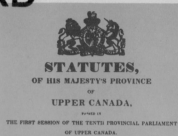

STATUTES,

OF HIS MAJESTY'S PROVINCE

OF

UPPER CANADA,

PASSED IN

THE FIRST SESSION OF THE TENTH PROVINCIAL PARLIAMENT

OF UPPER CANADA.

TO WHICH ARE PREFIXED,

AN ACT PASSED IN THE FOURTH SESSION, NINTH PROVINCIAL PARLIAMENT OF U. C. AS ASSENTED TO BY HIS MAJESTY;

AND CHAPS. LXXV. 6th. Geo. IV. AND LI. 6th. Geo. IV. IMPERIAL PARLIAMENT.

By Authority.

SIR JOHN COLBORNE, K.C.B.
LIEUTENANT GOVERNOR.

YORK, U. C.

PRINTED BY ROBERT STANTON — PRINTER — TO THE KING'S MOST EXCELLENT MAJESTY

King's College (University of Toronto) receives Royal Charter.

1828

Upper Canada College is founded.

Lord Dalhousie fails in attempt to veto Papineau as L.C. speaker.

W. L. Mackenzie elected to U.C. Assembly as member for York.

Canada Committee of British Parliament recommends widespread reform of Colonial government.

Date Due

BRODART, INC.   Cat. No. 23 233   Printed in U.S.A.

Margaret Atwood
Days of the Rebels
1815/1840

Canada's Illustrated Heritage

Canada's Illustrated Heritage

Publisher: Jack McClelland
Editorial Consultant: Pierre Berton
Historical Consultant: Michael Bliss
Editor-in-Chief: Toivo Kiil
Associate Editors: Michael Clugston
Harold Quinn
Jean Stinson
Assistant Editors: Rose Farrell
Marta Howard
Design: William Hindle
Lynn Campbell
Neil Cochrane
Cover Artist: Alan Daniel
Picture Research: Lembi Buchanan
Michel Doyon
Christine Jensen
Laurie McElhinney
Margot Sainsbury

ISBN: 0-9196-4416-3

N.S.L. Natural Science of Canada Limited
254 Bartley Drive
Toronto, Ontario M4A 1G4

Printed and bound in Canada

CHOLERA PREVENTIVE COSTUME.

This sketch shows the protective measures advised for doctors during the 1832 epidemic in the Canadas. Among other precautions, they were told to use nose covers, wear extra covering over all clothing, walk on tobacco leaves, and carry camphor and other herbs.

Contents

Members of the Tandem Club assemble for a frosty foray into the countryside outside Halifax, N.S. Buffalo robes, muffs and furs of all sorts went along for the ride. The top-hatted rubber-neckers outside Dalhousie College sport dashing trouser patterns: checks, horizontal and vertical stripes.

Ordinary People

The world is before me—a library open to all—from which poverty of purse cannot exclude me.

Joseph Howe, 1824

There were no ordinary people in the Halifax of 1815. There were only typical members of social classes. More than in any of the other British colonies, what you wore, what and when and how often you ate, where you lived, what you read and what you thought about what you read were all directly related to your social status. There was such an enormous gulf between the very rich and the very poor that the two groups thought of each other almost as members of different species. And there were classes within classes, distinctions within distinctions; even the smallest daily activities revolved around rank and precedent. A young girl not of the proper class who was seen walking with an officer would find her character ruined: everyone knew marriage between them was impossible. One old lady, remembering these days, recalled fondly how "the Bishop's lady once swept out of the ball-room with her daughters, because she saw the wife of a baker who had made money coming in at the door." Though the Halifax of 1815 was a small town by modern standards, it contained more variety in manners and dress than any North American city does today.

Young Joe Howe, who was a boy of ten at the time, must have found it an exciting place. Although he lived only two miles from the city, he could attend Mr. Bromley's co-educational school there only during the summer months, as at other times the road was impassable. After school he chased little girls on his way home, or played pitch-and-toss or marbles with other boys, or explored the city.

There were some streets where it was safer not to go. Halifax had both a harbour and a garrison, and it had been a wartime boomtown for longer than most of the adult inhabitants could remember. Now, just after the end of the War of 1812, it swarmed with sailors from the British navy, from the many privateers that towed their captured prizes into the harbour to be auctioned off, and from the merchant ships which traded with Britain and the West Indies. To service this traffic, whole sections of grog shops and "dancing houses" had grown up, where sailors fought and shouted and where "abandoned females of the lowest class, in a state of drunkenness, without shoes, and in the most filthy and abominable condition" sprawled or solicited. One street was called Barrack Street; another was Hogg Street, after a house of ill fame kept by a person of that name. Water Street and the Hill were slums, with dirty huts and shanties inhabited by even dirtier people. Little was done to control the riot, and respectable citizens had to

Catherine Parr Traill published this children's story, Little Downy; or, The history of a field-mouse: a moral tale, *in 1822. Her later, more candid works are chronicles of pioneer life in Upper Canada in the 19th century.*

lock their doors at night and take their washing off the line if a sailor was seen lurking about. There were no city police, courts or jail until 1815.

Needless to say, these portions of the city were smelly, vermin-ridden hotbeds of disease, venereal and otherwise. Water for the entire city was supplied by wells, which were easily polluted, especially in the slums. Garbage and slops were thrown into the gutters, where they stewed in hot weather. When it rained, the tainted water flowed downhill to the posh residential streets and seeped into the wells and cellars of the rich merchants and aristocratic British officers who lived in the mansions of Argyle Street. Though vaccination had been discovered, it was not widespread by 1815, and an epidemic of smallpox had swept through the city in the winter, killing poor and rich alike.

the latest London fashions

Joe Howe may have liked to walk along Argyle Street, with its clean, paved sidewalks and willow-lined, gravel-covered road-bed. The houses were of wood, for the most part, but, according to Bishop Plessis of Quebec, they were among the most attractive in the colonies, with "handsome porticoes, superb entrance doors and steps, broad stairways, and noble well-furnished apartments." Here officers in colourful uniforms went driving with ladies dressed in the latest London fashions, light slender dresses of muslin and summer bonnets of silk or straw. The rich merchants could almost compete with the gold-braided officers: Victorian blacks and drabs had not set in, and Beau Brummel still set the tone for clothes-conscious men. Trousers were skin-tight and worn over boots, with straps under the instep to stretch them still further. The favourite colour for the thin-waisted coats with their wide lapels was light blue, worn with brass buttons and starched cravats. A gentleman would show his wealth and taste by fes-

tooning himself with jewellery: silver or gold watches, still very expensive, with chains and fobs, rings, stickpins and, for an extra flourish, exquisite little snuffboxes. A gentleman would carry a silk handkerchief, to catch the sneezes.

On summer evenings, everyone, rich and poor alike, turned out to hear the open-air concerts of the regimental band. And every Sunday there was a grand parade, when the entire garrison, led by the Chief Justice in his scarlet and ermine robes and the admiral and general in gold lace, marched to St. Paul's Church. This church, of course, was Anglican. All those with power and social standing belonged to the "Established Church," and the only university in the province, King's College, was restricted to its members.

But Joe was probably more interested in the busy streets near the harbour and market. There he could watch the farmers in their heavy carts bringing their produce to market and the sailors unloading goods from the sailing ships that were already the foundation of Nova Scotia's economy.

news six months old

Joe was a voracious reader and went through as many English poems, plays and novels as he could get his hands on. About the only native literary products available then were the newspapers, and, looking them over, Joe may have thought he could do better. Those from the major colonial cities were alike in format and sometimes in content, since they made "extracts" from each other. There was little editorializing or commentary and nothing like the local travel sketches that were later to make Joe Howe famous. They consisted largely of government announcements, of advertisements for theatre performances and for the sale of houses, land, goods and drugs; and, sandwiched between, news of local calamities such as fires, robberies and drownings. The news from distant

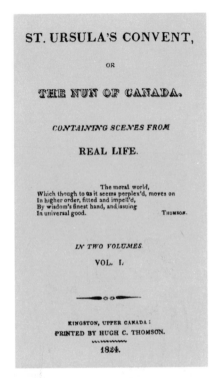

ST. URSULA'S CONVENT,

OR

THE NUN OF CANADA.

CONTAINING SCENES FROM

REAL LIFE.

The moral world,
Which though to us it seems perplex'd, moves on
In higher order, fitted and impell'd,
By wisdom's finest hand, and issuing
In universal good.   THOMSON.

IN TWO VOLUMES.
VOL. I.

KINGSTON, UPPER CANADA:
PRINTED BY HUGH C. THOMSON.
1824.

Julia Beckwith Hart of Kingston crafted this romantic tale in the popular style of the day – the first novel by a native English-Canadian.

lands–military defeats or victories and plagues–was often six months old when it was printed.

The biggest news in Halifax in the spring of 1815 was the signing of peace between the United States and Britain; it had taken three months to reach Halifax. No one, yet, anticipated the depression that would follow the end of the war. Halifax continued on its merry way, parading, dining and dancing, and making money hand over fist.

late loyalists and land-grabbers

In Upper Canada, at the other end of the settled British domain, the peace settlement was viewed with more alarm. Trade with the competitive States would now resume. A disgruntled correspondent in Kingston commented: "business. . . since the peace, has been exceedingly flat; and . . . the Americans have again commenced running in almost every description of their domestic manufacturers, such as leather, paper, hats and all their petty *notions*." Tories in York (Toronto), such as Upper Canada's Chief Justice William Dummer Powell, shared the fears of the British government about the American menace. Although the Yankees had burned a few buildings and made off with the town's fire engine, the citizens of York hadn't suffered that much from the recent invasion. The alarming thing was that some of the local people had joined in the looting and were thought to favour the American side. But what could you expect, with such a large number of "late loyalists" and land-grabbers in the neighbourhood? If the flow of Americans into Upper Canada was not checked soon, or at least balanced by an influx of loyal British subjects, Britain might lose the colony if there were ever another war. Those of Powell's circle were in favour of increased British immigration. Besides, it would be good for business. And more workmen, builders and skilled artisans would soon be needed. York had fought for its po-

SAINT JOHN THEATRE.

SECOND NIGHT of the GRAND MELO-DRAMA, called

TEKELI;

Or, The Siege of Montgatz.

On Wednesday Evening September 17, 1817,

Will be presented, (for the Second time,) the Grand Melo-Drama, in Three Acts, called

TEKELI;
Or, The Siege of Montgatz.

With New Scenery, Machinery, Decorations, &c. as performed upwards of 60 Nights in the Theatre Royal, London to overflowing Houses.—Written by Theodore Hook, Esq. Author of "The Fortress, &c."—With all the Original Music.

HUNGARIANS.   AUSTRIANS.

Count Tekeli,	Mr. PRICE.	Count Serassis, (the General,)	Mr. ALDIS.
Edmund, (his Lieutenant,)		Edmund, (his Lieutenant,)	Mr. CAREY.
Wolf, his Friend,)	Mr. ROBINSON.	Bras-de-Fer, (his Servant,)	Mr. PLACIDE.
		Maurice, (a town soldier,)	Mr. ARMSTRONG.
Citizens, Officers, Soldiers, &c.	By Supernumeraries.	Conrad, (a Miller,)	Mr. CHARNOCK.
		Ladyes, (his Son,)	Mr. KELLY.
		Frank,	Master EVERY.
		Christina,	Mrs. FOSTER.
	Miss AZELIA.	Alexina,	

Male and Female Peasants, &c.

ACT 1.—SCENE 1.   **REPRESENTS A FOREST.**

Time, Night.—On the right hand a large Oak, with other Trees in a clust. Tekeli is discovered lying on a Branch of the Oak which has fallen by age. His friend Wolf sleeping on the ground near him; on the left hand a cluster of small Trees. During the rise of the Curtain the last part of the Overture,

A STORM.

ACT 2.—SCENE 1.   **THE MILL OF KEBEN.**

The front filled with various Implements of Husbandry; Sacks of Flour are standing in different parts.   The whole of the centre open to the

RIVER TORZA.

On the right a practicable WIND MILL; on the left a WATER MILL, with Rolling Water, both Mills are in Motion

A WOODEN BRIDGE ACROSS THE TORZA,

Running from the right hand of the centre to the upper part of the Stage on the left.   The distant Country bounds the View The Peasants arrive with Tekeli on a Litter composed of Boughs who move with a warm and kind reception from the honest Miller. The incidents of this Act are interesting and innteresting; the business as interwoven with the disposition of the Scenery as to render the illusion as strong or stronger than any other scene in Dramatic representation.

ACT 3.—SCENE 1.   **A HALL.**

Alexina discovered on a Throne, &c.—Tekeli and Wolf arrive.—Tekeli calls for the Standard—Merrie—

For Freedom and Our Country,

SCENE LAST.   **THE FORTRESS OF MONTGATZ.**

With the extent of the Battlements, the Towers and Walls; on an elevated situation hangs the Hungarian Standard; a fire and Portcullis; a general conflict ensues. Edmund, the Austrian Lieutenant, seizes the Hungarian standard, and is bearing it off in Triumph, when Alexina meets him, and

A Combat between Alexina and Edmund

takes place—Tekeli enters, rescues Alexina—Edmund and Carafia's party fall—and Tekeli gives

FREEDOM TO HIS COUNTRY.

The Evening's Entertainment to conclude with the much admired *Farce*, in Two acts, called

The

Irishman in London.

Mr. Colloony,	Mr. ARMSTRONG.	Murtoch Delany,	Mr. PRICE.
Mr. Fitzroy,	Mr. CHARNOCK.		
Captain Seymour,	Mr. CAREY.	Louisa,	Miss YOUNG.
Edward,	Mr. ROBINSON.	Caroline,	Mrs. FOSTER.
Cymon,	Mr. PLACIDE.	Cubba,	Mrs. CHARNOCK.

Tickets, Five Shillings each, to be had of Mr. ALDIS, at the Theatre, where places may be taken.

British plays and troupes were common in the young Maritime cities. British army officers, avid for the theatre, organized most companies and productions.

**Young Joseph Howe
The Novascotian**

Joe Howe said of himself, "poetry was my first love but politics was the hag I married." He was the son of a Loyalist and had grown up at the printing press his father had brought with him from Boston. By age 24 he had been publisher and editor of the *Acadian Recorder* and had bought the *Novascotian*. For eight years he travelled the colony and printed sketches of places and people he visited. At the desk of his paper he wrote scathing articles attacking corruption and patronage. When he was sued for libel in 1835, he conducted his own defence and was acquitted after a six-hour speech. In 1836 he was elected to Assembly and launched a campaign that finally won responsible government for N.S. But Joe Howe never lost his love for writing: he was publisher of several authors, among them Haliburton, creator of the comic "Sam Slick."

sition as the seat of provincial government and, despite the grumblings of Niagara and Kingston, it intended to grow and prosper. Now that the war was over, people could give their energies to making improvements. Something needed to be done about the fire regulations, for instance; house fires were frequent, and the present system, leather buckets in every house, was next to useless. Schools and more churches would soon be needed. One had to make sure, though, that men with the proper loyalist views were in charge of them.

four o'clock dinner parties

Powell's grand-daughter, Mary, would have heard a good deal of political talk at the Chief Justice's dinner table, though, being a girl, she would not have been expected to pay too much attention to it. Instead she would have been required to help her grandmother, who had to entertain the notables of the town at dinners for sixteen twice a week. Mary, in her early teens in 1815, could already bake the puddings that were served as part of the second course. Although Mrs. Powell considered the one-storey frame house on Front Street woefully inadequate for the amount of entertaining she had to do, the Powells were far above the pork-and-potatoes level of the working classes. Her four o'clock dinner parties would have consisted of three courses, with their respective wines. The first would have been meats of various kinds: beef, pork, chicken, duck, goose, turkey, mutton, veal, lamb, and fish or venison in season; perhaps even some of the passenger pigeons that flew over in such great numbers that they menaced the farmers' crops. The second course would be fruit pies, puddings, custards, meat pies or mince pies in season. The third, a lighter course of fruit or dried fruit and nuts, was called "dessert." The menus of the day seem gluttonous, and having an ample figure was certainly no stigma; it meant that you

could afford to eat well enough to get fat. But not every guest would have a large helping of everything offered. The dishes for each course, instead of being passed around one at a time, as in the "Russian service" proper in mid-Victorian times, were all set on the table at once, and each guest helped himself to whatever he wanted.

When they were not eating dinner, members of Powell's circle were usually recovering from some other meal. Breakfast was at eight, a fairly large meal heavy in meat and eggs. Lunch was at twelve. After dinner at four there would be supper at seven or eight, which among the "higher classes" was known as "tea." At balls, a fifth meal called "supper" would appear at twelve or one.

the necessary wardrobe

In 1815, Mary Powell was looking forward to a great adventure. She was going to travel to New York to be "finished" at Miss English's Academy for Young Ladies. There was nothing so grand in York. Dr. Strachan thrashed the sons of the gentry at his school for boys, but there was no dependable school where a young lady might learn her French, drawing, embroidery and deportment. Outfitting Mary with the necessary wardrobe must have been troublesome too. Dresses were made at home by a dressmaker, but the cloth had to be bought. There were few specialty shops, and dry goods were sold in general stores, such as the one William Allan ran in partnership with Alexander Wood. Stores like theirs would have sold almost everything that could be bought: food, especially preserved and imported food, such as tea and sugar, boots and shoes, ladies' hats, soap and candles, guns, dress goods, china, nails, paint and tools, even a few books. Male customers could usually get a glass of whisky over the counter.

Doing business was tricky, since there was no universally used Canadian money. Buyers and sellers had to know the value of English pounds, American and Spanish dollars, Halifax and New York paper money, as well as the home-grown crops and the home-made items – hand-knit socks and mittens, homespun yarn, butter and cheese – that were offered by farmers in exchange for shop goods. There were no set prices in the store: everything was bargained for and haggled over. A shopkeeper had to give credit, or his customers – particularly those of the upper classes – would desert him for someone who would. Shopping, as well as shopkeeping, was a chancy affair. What a shop had in supply at any given time depended on the state of shipping, what had reached Montreal and what had made it, unbroken and unspoiled, on the four- to eight-week trip up the St. Lawrence and across Lake Ontario.

roads safe — when frozen

Simply getting to the shop was an ordeal in itself. It wasn't that the distances were great. York in 1815 had fewer than a thousand inhabitants. By Halifax and Montreal standards, it was little more than a wide place in the road. But it was the road, or rather the roads – Front and King, mainly – that added the spice of adventure to a simple shopping trip. They were only completely safe when they were frozen solid. They were unpaved, and when it rained carts and carriages would splash pedestrians with dirty water or bog down in the mudholes and ruts. People threw their garbage into the streets, where it was eaten by wandering pigs. Attempts were sometimes made to control the pigs, yoking them to keep them from burrowing through fences, and ringing their noses to make them easier to catch and lead away, but in view of the garbage it was just as well that so many of them got loose. A walk along the streets during the muddy season would have been out of the question for a lady and unpleasant for a gentleman.

Front Street was then the most distinguished part of town. Locations on the lakeshore were very desirable. Some town notables had once had the idea that every house there should be compelled to install pillars to improve the view from the harbour, though somehow this never got done. But even in the fashionable parts of town, the houses were a motley collection. Some lots still held the log cabins of the early settlers. Some were small frame houses where the town's many artisans and tradesmen lived: carpenters, joiners, cabinet makers, blacksmiths. All the houses, even those of the rich, were made of wood; brick did not become widely used for several decades. Most were enclosed by picket fences, to keep out the pigs, as well as the dogs and wandering cows and horses.

musical soirées

Even in these primitive surroundings, a rigid class structure was preserved. Some of the houses, referred to by their owners as "cottages," were large buildings more properly called mansions, with extensive lawns and grounds, carriage houses and stables. Here the government officials and their ladies, with the bungling aid of under-trained servants, attempted to re-create the leisurely life of the English privileged classes. Ladies and gentlemen paid morning visits, attended dinners, sang and played at musical soirées, and danced at balls. Men hunted and fished for recreation; both ladies and men enjoyed horseback riding, sleighing in winter, picnics in summer, and walks when it was not too muddy. York, like Halifax and every other principal town in the colonies, had a garrison nearby, and the officers and their wives figured prominently in the more prestigious social events. It was a pleasure-loving society if you were at the top, and Mary Powell, returning to it after two or three years of finishing, would have been eager to join in the fun.

SCHOOL FOR Young Ladies,
KINGSTON.

MR. & Mrs. TWIGG beg leave to return thanks for the liberal encouragement which they have received, and to acquaint their friends and the public that they continue to receive BOARDERS & DAY PUPILS, at their house in Quarry Street, where the following branches are as usual taught—

English and French Languages, Grammatically, *History, Geography, Composition, Music, Drawing, Dancing, Needlework, Writing and Arithmetic.*

From Mrs. Twigg's long experience, and the credentials which she has brought with her, (she having for many years conducted a similar establishment in her native country) they hope for a continuance of that support which they shall make it their study to merit.

Reference may be made to
The Rev. Archdeacon STUART,
Lieut. Col. MACPHERSON, and
Sheriff McLEAN.

Each young Lady to bring her bed, &c. &c. two pair of sheets and six towels.

August 18th, 1826.

Kingston's well-to-do families sent their daughters to schools like this, where the Twiggs advertised the best references in town. Before 1850, a few hundred youngsters in all of English Canada went beyond primary education. The sooner a girl was behind the spinning wheel and a boy ploughing the better. Education was only for the idle rich anyway.

Montreal harbour was the busiest in all of Canada in 1830, when this engraving was made. The steeple of Bonsecours Church was the beginning of a skyline. Tariffs bolstered the country's forest industry. Square-rigged ships are being loaded with square timber. An Indian's canoe skims the water toward a steamship.

CHAPTER ONE

A City of Two Tales

No, your great men are nothin' but rich men...
They were once all as poor folks as you be.

Thomas Chandler Haliburton, *The Clockmaker*, 1836

In 1815, Montreal was the largest, richest, most cosmopolitan city in the colonies. It was the centre of the fur trade, with its Nor 'Wester magnates and their sumptuous mansions sprouting on the side of the moutain in the district that would later be Westmount. It had a distinguished army garrison which had been of great military importance during the war and was of great social importance now that the war was over. It had a harbour, with many wharves lining the riverside and more being built. Here the trade goods and luxury items from England, the Continent, and the West Indies, such as mahogany furniture, mirrors, metal clocks, clothing, sweetmeats, wine, carpets and crystal, were unloaded. Here they were sold to the rich of the city and to merchants who would re-sell them at inflated prices, far in the interior, in Kingston with its pretensions and handsome architecture or in dumpy little York with its snooty government officials, its mosquitoes and mudholes. The merchants traded the other way, too, to England and the States. Their mansions also were spreading out, over land which had recently been the apple orchard of some habitant or petty seigneur glad to take advantage of the real-estate boom.

Montreal was one of the few places in the colonies, it was rumoured, where a gourmand could get a decent meal. And it was a tourist attraction, because it had that scarcest of North American commodities, age. It had stone buildings and tin roofs, which were thought to add to its picturesque charms. It also had nuns, three orders of them, habitants and their wives, who brightened up the marketplace with their blue homespun and their colourful caps and quilted bonnets, and voyageurs, with their air of daring romance. Here you could see everything and everyone: fashionable ladies in their carriages; Indians in their blanket coats and beadwork; visiting nobility; poor Scots Highlanders in their threadbare "plades," just off the boat. Quebec was older and more French, Fredericton considered itself more genteel, Halifax thought its high society was higher, but Montreal viewed itself as the hub of the northern part of the continent, and it was.

For all its Frenchness, it was a good place for an enterprising British merchant. A man could get rich here if he went about it in the right way, and many had. John Molson, for instance, had started out as an emigrant from Lincolnshire, and a mere brewer at that. But he'd learned French and, at the right time of year, he would put on a homespun suit, a blue tuque, and a pair of sabots, and stand outside his brewery, waylaying the small farmers on the way to the city with their wagons of grain.

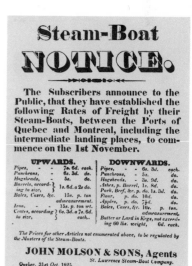

The Molson and Torrance companies dominated the steamboat service on the St. Lawrence. The first steamboat on the Montreal to Quebec run, the Accommodation, *built in 1809, cut sailing time between the two cities from fifteen days to three.*

He would so charm them with his bonhomie that they would sell to him rather than to his competitors; they nicknamed him "*le Père* Molson." He converted their grain into the already-famous Molson's Beer, which in 1815 sold for seven shillings and sixpence per dozen bottles.

Molson's Mansion House Hotel

Yet, despite his peasant act, *le Père* Molson had already amassed a small fortune, branched out into the grain business, and started a steamboat line. His steamboats, the *Accommodation,* the *Swiftsure* and the *Malsham,* were the first to run between Montreal and Quebec City. He was planning to go into the hotel business, too, and in December of 1815 he purchased "the House and extensive premises" of Sir John Johnson, Bart., where he was soon building and furnishing the Mansion House Hotel. In "extent and elegance" it was planned to be "the most complete Hotel in North America." It would have a ballroom 180 feet long and stabling for 70 horses; it would have a library and "News Room," for the reading of newspapers, to which the colonials were known to be addicted. It would also have some smaller ballrooms, some supper rooms and card rooms, with two "Dressing Rooms adjoining, fitted up in a style which cannot fail to give satisfaction." The chandeliers alone cost more than a thousand pounds, an astronomical sum for those days. Mr. Molson hadn't done badly for a man of humble farmer stock, and the weekly newspaper, the four-page *Montreal Herald,* regarded him with approbation. "If he has made a handsome fortune," it commented, "he well deserves it; and the public has a deep interest in the success of all his enterprizes." The paper reported not only on the movements of his steamboats, but on the movements of his radishes, which were also considered to be news: "On Sunday last (March 26) Mr.

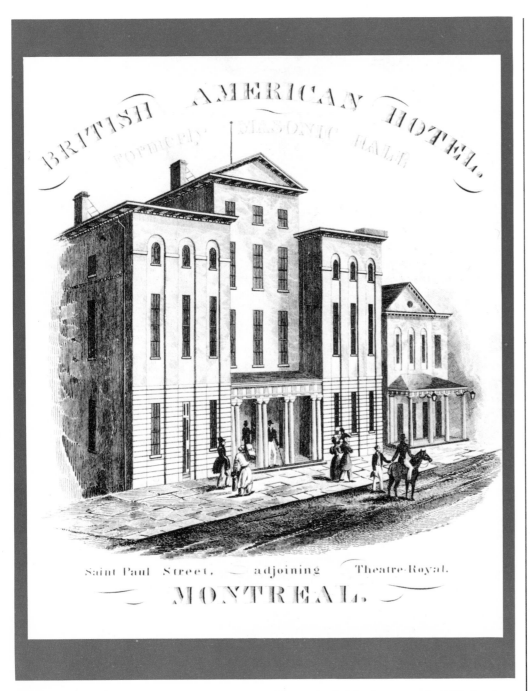

The British-American Hotel faces a muddy St. Paul Street flanked by flagstones. In 1833 the place went up in flames, a common disaster: bucket brigades were little more help than spectators.

M'Kenzie, Gardener to John Molson, Esqur. presented to his employer about 6 dozen fine Radishes, perfectly matured for the table."

Molson, being a tradesman, would not have been considered a member of the crème de la crème of society. Still, he was a leading citizen of Montreal, and a very rich one. In 1814 he had switched from the Presbyterian Church to the Anglican, a step up the religious social ladder. Social distinctions were blurring slightly around the edges even in Europe as merchants crept into the aristocracy and aristocrats gambled away their fortunes, and the Molsons would have gained the entrée almost everywhere. Sarah Molson was equal to the station to which Providence and the shrewd trading sense of her husband had called her. She was of a respectable family and was doubtless considered, back in England, to have married a little beneath herself. Molson and his three sons conducted the business, while Mrs. Molson would have run the household and fulfilled her duties as the wife of such a prominent man by engaging in the social life of the city.

The Marquis' Masquerade

There was a lot, in those years after the war, to keep Montreal's wealthier citizens busy. The most spectacular social events were the balls, and the most prestigious balls were given by such luminaries as the Marquis of Tweedale or by the officers of the garrison, though lesser souls such as the tradesmen also had their balls. The Marquis threw his Masquerade in the winter of 1815, for over two hundred guests. They wore costumes meant to represent Indian women, nuns, Irishmen, servants, peasants, and other droll creatures. Guests danced until one in the morning, when they took off their masks and had supper, "where all the delicacies of the first *Maître de Cuisine* were laid out in a style seldom before witnessed in this country." At dawn

they promenaded through the streets in their costumes, "to the wonder of the industrious peasant, as he came to market."

elegant . . . but smelly

The balls given by different regiments of the garrison were also much admired. The Bachelor Officers of De Meuron's Regiment opened 1816 by inviting their fellow officers and the principal inhabitants of the city to their "elegant BALL & SUPPER," for which they had decorated their mess hall with mirrors and evergreen branches, "fancifully arranged," and festooned the ceiling with "drapery of various colours. . . which had a very pleasing effect." Sometime, for these balls, the windows were covered with "transparancies," pictures or designs lit from behind. There was one thing about these balls which the society notes didn't mention. They were smelly. The heat from the candles and fireplaces emphasized the fact that baths after October were viewed as highly imprudent, even among the upper classes, and although perfume was used to offset the aroma it must still have been overpowering.

Mrs. John Molson, who was a matron of fifty-five by this time, would probably not have danced for the full eight hours; that kind of strenuous exercise was reserved for the unmarried girls, who might wear out one pair of low-heeled satin or kid dancing slippers a night. The Bachelor Officers, unlike their counterparts thirty years later, would actually have been able to see the feet of their partners, as skirts had not yet descended to Victorian level. Necklines were low, waists were high, sleeves were short and worn with long gloves, and skirts, not yet stiff with crinolines, were narrow. The favourite colour for young ladies was white, set off with gold or silver embroidery. Mrs. Molson would probably have chosen a darker colour, a higher neckline, and a shawl. In fact, she must have found the modern

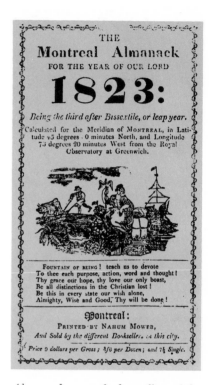

Almanacks were the bestsellers of the period. About 50 were put out early in the century in Lower Canada, and Nahum Mower's was one of the best. The Massachusetts native came to Montreal in 1807 and operated his printing office until his death in 1830.

Old Montreal

Montreal in 1815. Surrounded by miles of forest wilderness, there sat the city poking steeples, monuments, domes, crosses and carved pediments at the sky. These might catch a traveller's eye as he disembarked at a harbour still free of industrial clutter. Then on to straight avenues fringed, in some cases, with board sidewalks, and in the richer neighbourhoods lined with houses made from the island's grey limestone. Many sewers were already covered, and gloomy iron shutters of an earlier, violent era had been replaced with more elegant wood. One visitor noted "a commendable absence of all meretricious style and ornament." But not all was rosy. Limestone dust from the streets was part of a Montrealer's summer diet, and rain could turn the avenues into impassable mud. The break with the forest was gradual: fields and orchards stretched away up from the city gates to the mountain.

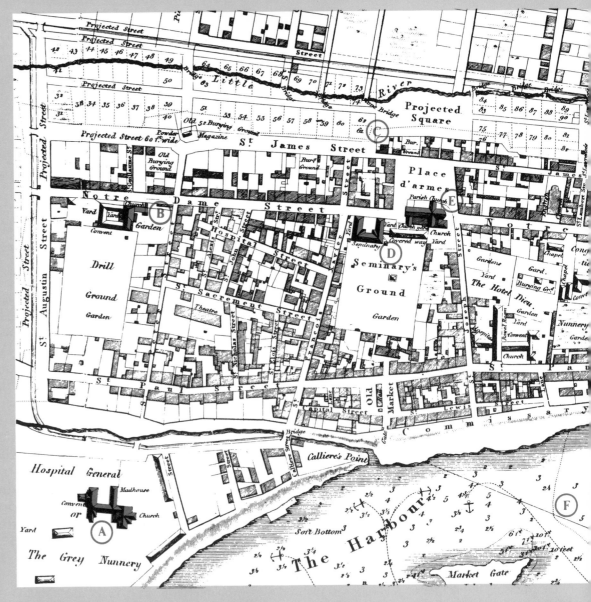

A Grey Nunnery

B Recollect Church

C Bank of Montreal

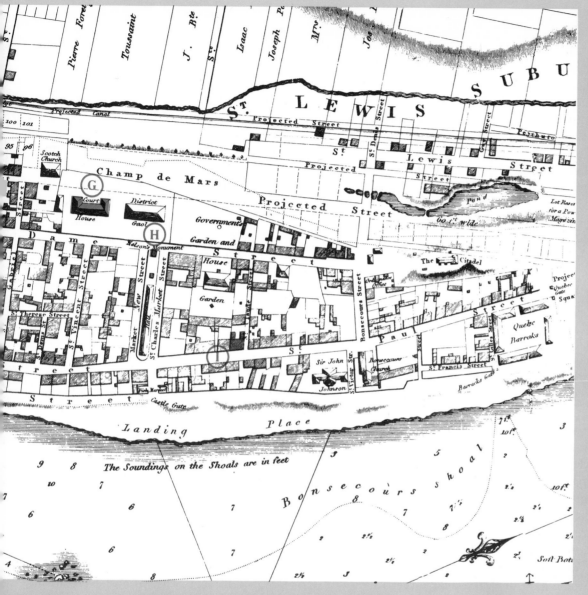

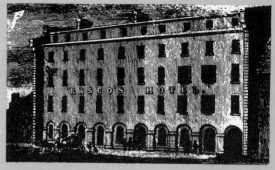

I Rasco's Hotel

H Nelson's Monument

G Court House

D Seminary

E Place d'armes

F City of Montreal from the harbour

Ezekiel Hart
The Politician Who Never Was

Ezekiel Hart was a Jew. He was born in Trois Rivières in 1770, where his father Aaron, a merchant, had settled. There were less than 100 Jews living in British North America at the time, and when Ezekiel decided to try his hand at politics, his father and his friends thought he was crazy. Little is known of his political views, but in Quebec in 1807 he was the focus of a controversy that took 25 years to settle. In the election that year he won a seat in the legislature of Lower Canada, but was not allowed to take office while judges debated to establish whether a Jew, who could not take the oath "on the true faith of a Christian," should be granted the rights of other citizens. In 1832 the matter was finally settled, and his son, Samuel, was the first Jew to hold a seat in a British legislature.

style of dress distasteful. Not only did the girls go practically naked to balls, but the dresses they wore in the daytime were hardly any better. The wars and revolutions of recent years, the introduction of that immodest dance, the waltz, and the influence of Napoleon's scandalous court had made young ladies rather daring. Some even recited Byron.

It was difficult to be absolutely up to the minute in fashion, though, since the current London styles were not described in the Montreal papers until three months later. The April fashions for 1815, which reached Montreal in July, featured "the Anglo-Persian hat, with plumes of ostrich feathers . . . Turkish gauze dress over white satin . . . Primrose kid shoes and gloves." For morning, there was a simpler outfit of salmon taffeta, with a satin bonnet in "evening primrose," a matching pelisse, and blue kid gloves and shoes. For evening, it would be appropriate to wear your pearl or diamond earrings, if you had any.

frilled underdrawers

Undergarments, too, were imported, by such traders as Keene & Co., who in 1816 received 300 pairs of "CORSETTS, of the newest shapes." The "Respiration Stays" were particulary recommended. The straight skirts required only one petticoat, and some women wore none. Frilled underdrawers were a thing of the future; some women didn't even bother with stockings, though in a Montreal winter you would have to wear a thick layer of fur over this flimsy costume to keep from freezing to death. And beaver bonnets, though they were made from Canadian beavers, were also shipped from England. Montreal sent out the raw pelts; the English mixed the thick waterproof under-fur with the hair of other animals, such as rabbits, then pressed the fur into felt and shaped it into winter hats for men, women and children.

But young ladies of the richer classes had more

than dancing and clothes to amuse them. In winter there were sleighing parties, again with the officers of the garrison. The officers also provided most of the theatrical entertainment in town. Once a week, during the winter season, the "Amateurs of the Garrison" put on a play, usually a light comedy followed by an "after-piece," such as "Miss in her Teens." These performances were well attended, and the "laughter-loving audience" had the satisfaction of knowing that the proceeds were applied to "Charitable Purposes." There was theatre in French, too, performed by La Société des Jeunes Messieurs Canadiens at Tessyman's Hotel; they sometimes did Molière.

the education of a young lady

Musical young ladies could purchase their "new music for the Piano Forte, Songs, etc.," as well as their violin strings and tuning forks, from Mr. Holland, and a Mr. Fred Glackmeyer, Jr., imported pianofortes, flutes, and "a great number of other articles in this line, too tedious to detail." Drawing and embroidery were practised by the young ladies of Montreal as well as by those of Europe, and several schools, such as Mrs. Knight's, which also taught Geography, Writing, and Arithmetic, existed to instruct them.

Mrs. Molson had no daughters to educate, and she already knew how to embroider. But there would be parties and special festivals to plan: New Year's Day, for instance, when almost everyone in the city, especially the French and the Scots, went calling. Plenty of food and, especially, drink would have to be set out for the men who would arrive in their sleighs and carioles to kiss the ladies, drink their health and eat some cakes and sweetmeats before going on to the next house.

Much of Mrs. Molson's time would have been spent supervising the preparation and preservation of the huge amounts of food required by her large establishment. Her domain would have been equipped with an ice-house, for storing meat and perishables in the summer, and a cool cellar, lined with brick or stone, for storing bacon and hams, root vegetables and fruit. This was particularly crucial in Montreal, since it was on an island completely cut off from the mainland when the river was freezing in the fall and breaking up in the spring. Unlike many refined ladies of the latter half of the century, who considered their stomachs to be unmentionable and who prided themselves on their ignorance of food, Mrs. Molson would have cared about the quality of her table. She may not have been above baking the odd cake or confection herself, and, like many women of her generation and class, she may even have kept a scrapbook where her thoughts and the treasured letters of her friends were inserted side by side with her favourite recipe for pickle or pudding.

Wanted, a female servant

She would have supervised the gardening as well. Many people had their own vegetable and flower gardens; some, like the Molsons, had a gardener too. There were fields close to the city and even in it, where you could rent garden space and pasturage for your cows if you didn't have room on your own property. The Montreal Florist Society, a very active body devoted to the cultivation of almost everything, gave advice on insects and blights and donated plants to new settlements. They had an annual grape and melon show, and in 1815 the Molsons' gardener took second prize for the grapes and firsts for the "finest flavoured Musk Melon," and his fourteen-pound watermelon.

Mr. M'Kenzie would not have been the Molsons' only servant. Even lower-middle-class families kept at least one servant, usually female. An advertisement in the *Herald* put the needs of such families in the plainest terms:

Wanted, a Female Servant of good character, who understands Cooking and the Drudgery of the House. A Woman having a child will not answer.

The Molson servants would have been more specialized. There would have been a butler, to manage the wine. (For drinking water, the Molsons may have used bottled Saratoga mineral water, imported from the States. Water for washing was delivered in barrels and was not very sanitary.) The cook would have been a good one, with a kitchen-maid to help her, and she would have had the best equipment, perhaps even one of the new-fangled wood-burning iron ranges, though probably she would still have been cooking with a brick oven and an open fireplace. Iron stoves were used mostly for heating rooms at this time, and only by the wealthier families.

Then there was the heavy work: scrubbing the floors, beating the carpets, doing the wash in huge pots heated over a fire. Someone, too, would have had to empty the chamber pots, though the Molsons may have had one of Wisely and Moor's water-closets. Polishing the stoves, cleaning them out, lighting the fires, and cleaning the chimneys, which caught fire if they were allowed to fill with soot, was just part of the normal "drudgery of the house."

the twilight world

Commentators agreed that, in the colonies, a good servant was hard to find. Back in England, with its surplus population and starving poor, servants counted themselves lucky even if they had to slave from morning to night and they did so without complaint. They did not talk back to their employers, and they did not leave their positions on the chance of getting better ones. If they were dismissed without a reference, they were not likely to find another position. Women sacked by their em-

Etienne Parent
Editor of *Le Canadien*

In Quebec, where the printed word and politics were never far apart, young Etienne Parent found himself the arbiter of culture and public opinion. He was born in Beauport, L.C., in 1801, and after editing the journal, *Le Canadien,* from 1822 to 1825, he left his desk to study law. When he revived the paper six years later, it appeared under the banner, *"Nos institutions, notre langue, nos lois."* His own politics came into conflict with those of the militant and radical *patriotes,* and up to the eve of the rebellion, his editorials prophesied years of repression to follow the ill-timed uprisings. Nevertheless, he spent five months in prison in 1838 for denouncing the suspension of civil rights, and throughout the 1840's was active in repairing the damage done in the days of the rebels.

The Brandy Trade

Nova Scotia's "Brandy Dispute" caught customs officials flat-footed. In a battle over the import duty of brandy, the government let the old duty lapse, and before it could set a new rate, importers had whiskied in a fortune in duty-free booze. Enos Collins, both an importer and councilman, profited by delaying the tax bill in the legislature.

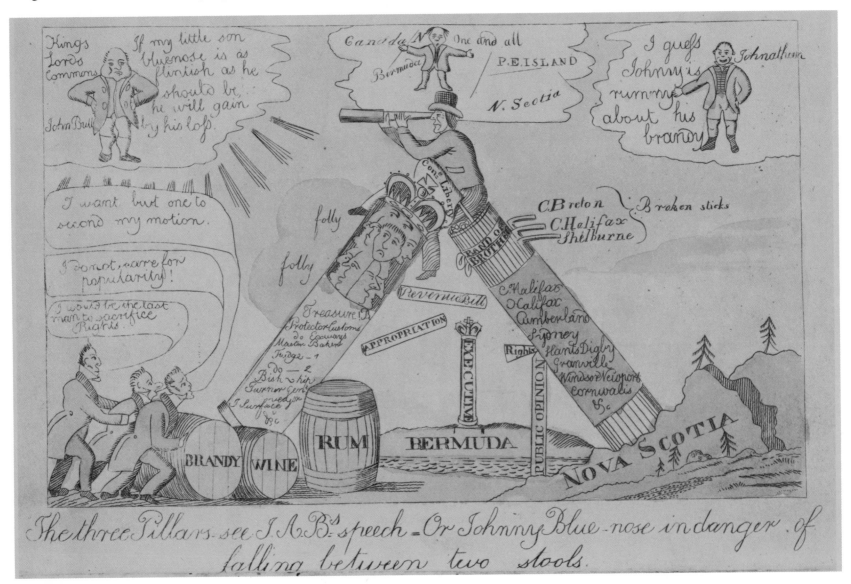

ployers would descend to the twilight world of prostitutes, drunkards and thieves. Servants in England cringed because they had to.

In the New World it was different. The United States was a hotbed of republicanism, and immigrants to the Canadas were tainted by proximity. They couldn't seem to get it into their heads that, as they were still under British rule, British customs should prevail. As soon as they were off the boat, they became uppity. Susanna Moodie warned her readers against bringing servants across the Atlantic and paying for their passage: they would only desert as they soon discovered that "help" was in demand, and that in the more remote areas they had much more bargaining power than at home. Even on the ship they indulged in great expectations: "The poorest and the worst-dressed, the least deserving and the most repulsive in mind and morals exhibited most disgusting traits of self-importance. . . . Girls, who were scarcely able to wash a floor decently, talked of service with contempt, unless tempted to change their resolution by the offer of twelve dollars a month." Their hopes were a little high. In 1826, according to Catherine Parr Traill, a servant girl might get a pound a month. A "serving lad" would get double that, and a full-grown male servant four times as much. By English standards these wages were considered exorbitant, and, in addition, employers would often be "subjected to great inconvenience from the spirit of equality and independence which subsists among the lower classes."

the lower class of people

But that was in Upper Canada, and to get there you first had to pass through Lower Canada. Things were different there. Quebec and, especially, Montreal were crowded with poor immigrants, many of whom could not yet afford the journey west to York. In Upper Canada there were more

positions than servants, but Montreal was a buyer's market. In 1817, the *Montreal Herald* carried an unusually long article headed "Distress of the Lower Class of People." Some benevolent gentlemen had counted up the number of those in "actual distress," that is, starving and freezing. They had found fifteen hundred. "The distressing scenes in many families," the paper commented, "are truely heart-rending."

babies and wet nurses

It was not for nothing that tourist guides referred to Montreal as the continent's most "European" city, and woman servants there were subjected to the usual European conditions, including the tacit understanding that they were sexually available to their male employers. While the young ladies in their white dresses danced with the officers, a different kind of sexual drama was being played out in the kitchens and back hallways. And prospects for a pregnant servant were bleak. If she had a child, it would be even harder to get a job; a woman with a child would usually "not answer." She might become a wet nurse, as mothers of the upper classes, in Montreal as in England, considered it *déclassé* to nurse their own babies. But many babies were left on the steps of the Hôtel Dieu for the nuns to take care of. Sometimes the results were even more tragic. A month before the newsworthy radishes nourished by the Molsons' gardener appeared on the dinner table, another small item had appeared in the Montreal paper:

A most atrocious deed has been lately perpetrated . . . . A Servant Girl who had managed to conceal her pregnancy feigned to be indisposed, and being in a chamber by herself, was delivered of a child which was afterwards found in the stove by another servant, partly consumed.

John Molson
Father of a Dynasty

John Molson stepped off a boat from England in 1782, an orphan at age 18. In the next half-century he turned his energies to building a business empire, a closely-knit family, and to improving Montreal's business life. Molson's brewery is his most famous legacy, but he also dominated shipping on the St. Lawrence and Ottawa, owned hotels in Montreal and Quebec City, and had a hand in many other enterprises. He used to dress as an habitant and greet French-Canadian farmers in *patois,* but his honest dealings won their trust and business. He introduced steamboats for travel in Lower Canada, and his taste for finery insured that his boats were fitted with the best of everything. In 1832 he won election to the Legislative Council of the colony. His death in 1836 (of "quack pills," his family said) was mourned in French and English papers.

Cutting Ice on the St. Charles River *(1830) caught clusters of ice sellers haggling with customers over prices—a century before refrigerators.*

Lieutenant Cockburn's Canada

"These sketches were originally done to while away some part of the idle hours of a soldier's life abroad . . . ," wrote an army officer stationed in Halifax in 1837. He, like Lt. James Cockburn, was doing his tour of duty in "the colonies," and like many other career soldiers found Canada a land of fascinatingly different subjects and scenes. Until the uprisings of 1837, an average day in the life of an officer was hardly rigorous. Part of the day was occupied with drills and reviews, surveys, map-making and miscellaneous business. Afternoons and evenings were for entertainments, concerts, banquets and balls, or calling on the respectable (and sometimes not so respectable) young ladies in town. But there was plenty of free time to see the sights, and officers with an eye for detail and colour often passed the hours sketching city scenes and land and seascapes. Lt. Cockburn arrived in Quebec in 1827, and by the time he left Canada five years later, he had created a remarkable visual record of the scenic wonders and everyday curiosities in colonial Canada.

The launching of the steamer, Royal William, *was an historical event not to be missed.*

Lt. Cockburn's Quebec was a city of contrasts. Goats graze along the cliffs above Lower Town.

Joseph Légaré painted this ghoulish scene of the 1832 cholera epidemic in Quebec City. The flames in front of houses are burning tar—believed to purify the air.

CHAPTER TWO

The Fiery Sword

How great the ardour which their souls inspired,
Who, leaving far behind their native plain,
Have sought a home beyond the western main.

Oliver Goldsmith, "The Rising Village," 1825

Year after year the emigrants poured across the Atlantic. They came by the hundreds, by the thousands and finally by the millions: between 1800 and 1875, more than 7,500,000 people left for the New World from the British Isles alone. By 1828, thirty thousand a year were crossing. They came in large ships and in small ships, in sound ships and in ships so rotten that they sometimes sank before they were out of sight of Britain. They came in the comfortable and expensive cabins, and they came jammed like sardines into the holds of returning timber ships that were not designed to carry human beings at all. Some of the emigrant ships had been built for the slave trade, but slaves were a valuable cargo whose costs could be regained only when they were sold alive. Emigrants, on the other hand, paid half their passage in advance; they were therefore more expendable, and in some ways worse treated. In 1831, the *Airthy Castle* docked in Quebec, carrying 254 passengers. She was 116 feet long. In 1829, the 90-foot *Vestal* arrived in Charlottetown, with 301 passengers.

People emigrated because they had to. In Scotland, those who owned the land, the lairds or those who had bought the lairds out, found that sheep were more profitable than people. The Highland clansmen, who had lived in the same glen for twenty or even forty generations, were driven away. Many went to the Canadas because they had no other place to go. The weather, too, played a part. The summer of 1816 was cold and wet, crops failed, and famine forced many out. The English middle classes and tradesmen, too, were hard hit by the end of the Napoleonic Wars. Many petty officers and soldiers were out of work and had no other career to fall back on. In Ireland, hunger was habitual. The potato famine had not yet struck, but thousands were leaving anyway. The British government encouraged emigration; they'd seen, during the War of 1812, that the loyalty of the American squatters along the Canadian borders was questionable. They wanted to flood the countryside with British emigrants so this problem wouldn't arise again.

One anonymous nineteenth-century writer, talking about emigration, spoke of "the conquering energy of a host of nameless men and women driven out into misery by the fiery sword of economic pressure, to eat their bread in strange places, and to bear their children in sorrow, that through them the men of the future may subdue nature and inherit the earth." This was fine rhetoric and gave a kind of biblical sanction to what was from first to last a shoddy business. The hosts *were* nameless; so much was true. But they left

A British newspaper lampoons the "riff-raff" that emigrated to British North America by the thousands, distressing "respectable" settlers.

Abysmal poverty, the failure of the potato crop, and fever left thousands of Irish tenants unable to pay their rents and keep food on the table. When landlords turned them out, those who could manage the fare crossed the Atlantic for Canada.

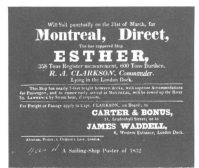

"Coppered" ships had metal plates below the waterline to protect timbers from rot. But passengers had little protection against dishonest captains and cholera. Because of strong opposition, the British government rescinded orders that emigrant ships should be provided with a surgeon, a medicine chest, and that bedding be cleaned daily during the voyage.

with no sense of conquering energy. For the most part they were impelled not by such stirring motives but by despair. They were not driven out of a kind of Garden of Eden into misery: Britain was no paradise for them, and, although it pained them to leave their homes, they were already in misery. They were bearing their children in sorrow anyway. And they were less likely to feel that they were subduing nature than that nature, through disease and famine, had already subdued them. The fiery sword that drove them was not the Angel of God or even some abstract "economic pressure": it was the greed and rapacity of other men. The emigrants' one hope was that they might inherit, if not the earth, at least a small patch of land. In Britain, only the rich owned land. In the colonies, it was said, even a poor man might, by hard labour and perseverance, obtain a little land that he could actually *own,* not rent or work for someone else. This was the one thing that would make the voyage worth it.

That is, if you could survive the voyage. Many didn't. For poor men or women, the voyage across the Atlantic in the steerage of a sailing ship (and most ocean ships before 1840 were sailing ships) was likely to be as close to hell as they would ever come. Transporting emigrants was big business, and many got rich on it; as in a lot of businesses, the unscrupulous took advantage of the gullible and the desperate. The more people you could cram into your ship, the more fares you could collect. The less you spent on repairs and supplies, the more you could spend on yourself. Emigrant-shippers were the slum landlords of the early nineteenth century, and in many cases being on one of these boats was worse than being in a jail, even a jail of that time.

One book for emigrants gave the following advice, which was, however, too little followed:

Parties going together in the steerage, or half-deck, would do right in closely examining into the exact

You had to be made of stern stuff to survive a crossing in the steerage of a "coffin" ship: dank, dark, stinking compartments, over-run with lice, fleas and rats, where food was old and uncooked, and cutpurses enjoyed easy picking.

16 or 18 pecks of Potatoes, in a barrel *with a lock* upon it.
40 lb. of good beef, well salted in brine, *with a lock* upon it.
16 lb. of butter.
3 lb. of coffee.
3 or 4 doz. *old* bottled beer, which has less chance of *flying* than if new.
Some dozens of eggs, packed in salt.
½ doz. cod fish, cut in pieces for boiling.
Some dozens of Buckie haddocks, well dried for keeping.
Milk does not keep well.
No sweetmeats are relished at sea.
A few oranges, which at times taste very pleasant to the parched palate.
Some cheese.
8 lb. of treacle, in a flaggon.
1 stone of barley–a good deal of pepper and mustard.
Plenty of carrots, turnips, and onions, for broth; they will keep all the voyage.
28 lb. of fine ship bread.
8 or 10 quartern loaves, baked hard, from Matthews.
1 boll of oatmeal, 6 pecks baked into bannocks and cakes, very well fired, and flat for packing.
Some white puddings.
Some suet for dumplings.
A few candles, and a white-iron lanthern with horn.
1 bottle of vinegar, to use in water on shipboard.
1 do. of castor oil, and some oz. of colocynth, and rhubarb pills.
6 lb. of Epsom salts, and 1 lb. senna. These medicines are very dear here.
Tin pan to fit the stove in the ship, and it is convenient to have one for hooking on the ribs of the grate, when the top of the fire is occupied.
Kettle for making coffee, &c.

This food list, recommended for four steerage passengers, was wildly unrealistic. Most steerage budgets ran mainly to oatmeal and potatoes.

accommodations they are to receive, such as water-closets; if they are to be allowed the use of the quarter-deck at sea;... these cautions may prevent bad feelings on the passage....

The same message echoes over and over through these books; inspect the ship yourself. Ask around. Trust no one. You could be defrauded before you even got on board. Ports swarmed with con-men and sharpers out to dupe the poor. In addition to the touts for rotten ships, you might be accosted by men who would sell you a ticket for a ship that didn't even exist or by those who, working in concert with a lodging-house keeper, would lie about a ship's date of departure. You'd have to wait around for weeks, while your lodging-house keeper billed you and the port merchants charged you outrageous prices.

Once you had set sail, there was no turning back. You would already have sold what little property you might possess in order to pay for your fare and for your food for the voyage. Your fare would have been cheap enough, as low as thirty shillings, but what it bought you was miserable. The berths in steerage ran along the sides of the ship and were two or sometimes three tiers high, with only a couple of feet between them. Your bed would be a rough wooden plank, six feet long and three feet wide. Although the shipowner might tell you before sailing that this was for you alone, you would find once under way that you had to share it with another person. There were often no separate quarters for married couples, no partitions for single women. You provided your own bedding. The chests with belongings and provisions were ranged in a line between the berths and used as tables or seats. Only the best ships provided real tables.

If the ship was a timber ship which had come from Montreal full of squared timbers, the berths would be temporary, tacked up for the return journey to be dismantled again on arrival. Sometimes

**Rev. William Bell
A Pioneer Preacher**

When this Scots Presbyterian pastor arrived in Perth, U.C., with his wife and six children, he found two houses, 30 log cabins and some tents were his parish. His first service was held in the loft of the local inn, but in two years the town boasted a new church. He was a man of any and every trade: carpenter, doctor, vet, teacher. He built houses and roads; delivered babies and introduced new and successful vaccines and medicines to the community; and opened school in his own rough cabin. In 1832 Bell organized the first temperance society in the area, and one of the first in the country. All in all, he earned every farthing of his $100 annual pay. His two books, *Hints To Immigrants* and his *Journal,* give a frank account of the "trials and tribulations" of a pioneer preacher in the backwoods.

the wood was rotten and the berths collapsed en route. On the *Ceres,* two children were killed when this happened; on the *Rothiemurchus,* a berth collapsed during a storm while a woman was being delivered of a premature baby, but the consequences were not quite so fatal. If you were a woman with small children, they slept with you on your narrow plank, and this could be dangerous too. If the ship wallowed or listed suddenly, you might crush your own children to death.

dismal conditions in steerage

Even in fairly calm weather, the steerage was a noisy place. A preacher named Bell described his first night out:

When the evening approached, a good deal of noise and confusion took place before all the passengers were arranged in their berths; and the Captain was obliged to interpose his authority, and to determine which bed every one was to have. This was an arrangement which ought to have been made sooner, and the want of it occasioned much unnecessary trouble, both to the Captain and passengers. We now began to feel what it was to be at sea with so much company. The crying of the children, the swearing of the sailors, and the scolding of the women who had not got the beds they wanted, produced a concert in which it was difficult to discover any harmony. Its disagreeable effect was heightened by the darkness of the night, and the rolling of the ship; which, at this time, began to be agitated by a sea somewhat rough.

During a storm, the noise would have been deafening. Chests and baggage might break loose and go crashing around with every roll of the ship. The thunder of the waves against the hull was much louder than in the cabins above. And the crying of children and the screams of terrified passengers, most of whom had never been on a ship before in their lives, would have been alarming. Sometimes

the screams were justified, since the ship was actually sinking.

Considering the dismal conditions in the steerage, it's remarkable that the passengers occasionally managed to enjoy themselves. Mr. Bell conducted services every Sunday, twice a day, during which everyone sang hymns and Mr. Bell prayed and read Scripture. He was gratified at the first service that "not an instance of levity was observed during the whole time." If the passengers were Scots, they would have their piper along, and if there was a fiddler, there might even have been dancing and music amidships. One cabin passenger complained to his friends that he had not enjoyed the voyage because of the noise from the steerage. It isn't clear whether he meant the music or the screams.

cholera, dysentery, typhus

The steerage was smelly, dark, and unhealthy. Often the steerage passengers were not allowed out, or their time on deck was rationed. Some captains made them air their bedding on deck, where it was occasionally blown away, but usually sanitation was minimal. Water even for drinking was scarce, and to use it for washing was out of the question. From the moment he embarked, a steerage passenger in a bad ship would be surrounded by the stench of bilge, vomit, smoke from what little cooking would be done on charcoal braziers or small stoves, decaying food, and human excrement. In such close quarters, disease was common. Cholera, dysentery and typhus, once on board, often ran through the entire ship.

But disease wasn't the only cause of death. A favourite ship-owner's trick was to lie to the emigrants about the length of the voyage and also about the amount of food they would need. The emigrant would plan for a four-week trip, but if the voyage lasted five, six or even seven weeks – as

Epidemic

The cholera epidemic of 1832 killed 7,000 people in the Montreal and Quebec City areas. But it wasn't the only threat to health and life. Smallpox, typhus, influenza, malaria and tuberculosis also took heavy tolls in the British colonies.

RETOUR DE L'HOTEL DIEU.

Retour des Malades admis dans l'Hotel Dieu depuis le 1er. Juillet jusqu'au 1er. Octobre 1833.

Dans l'Hôpital le 1er. Juillet.... 31 } 128
Admis durant les trois mois..... 97 }
Déchargés, Guéris 65, Soulagés, 24..89 }
Morts.......................10 } 128
Maintenant dans l'Hôpital..........29 }
Catholiques..93   Protestans......35..128

MALADIES ADMISES.

Phrénésie,	2	Céphalolgie,	1
Pneumonie,	11	Anasarque,	3
Gastrite,	1	Ascites,	1
Entérite,	1	Hydro-thorax,	2
Iritis,	1	Jaunisse,	1
Hépatite,	4	Consomption,	8
Rhumatisme,	8	Embarras Gastriques	12
Pemphigus,	1	Aménorrhée,	2
Dyssenterie,	4	Pléthore,	1
Paralysie,	3	Varice,	1
Dyspepsie,	1	Sarcome,	1
Chlorose,	3	Hydarthrose,	8
Palpitation,	2	Morsure,	1
Pyroxis,	1	Blessures,	5
Hystérie,	1	Ulcères,	9
Abies,	3	Nécrose,	1
Contusion,	2	Fracture de la jambe,	2
Teigne,	2	Lacération,	1
Dartres,	2	Débilité,	1

Dans deux cas de lacération trois doigts ont été amputés.

Il n'y a que 35 lits de montés dans l'Hôpital et il y en a eu jusqu'à 9 de vides à la fois, faute de demandans.

W. A. HALL.

A patient's faith and illness are noted on this sick list.

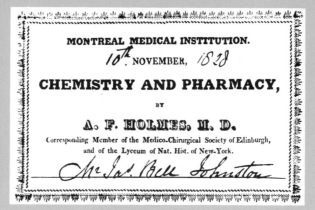

MONTREAL MEDICAL INSTITUTION.
10th. NOVEMBER, 1828
CHEMISTRY AND PHARMACY,
BY
A. F. HOLMES, M. D.
Corresponding Member of the Medico-Chirurgical Society of Edinburgh, and of the Lyceum of Nat. Hist. of New-York.

Mr Jas. Bell Johnston

Whiskey was prescribed if chemicals and medicines failed.

CHOLERA BULLETIN.
Printed at the Wesleyan Office.

TO the President of the Board of Health of the Gore District:

Sir----I have this morning received a communication from Doct. GILPIN of Brantford, stating he was called to visit Three cases, which he considers exhibited characters of Spasmodic Cholera. One case, a man by the name of *Young*, proved fatal in 8 hours. The other two were convalescent when Doctor Gilpin writes.

The following is a report I submit to the Board of Health, on the above cases.

Cases of *CHOLERA* in the Gore District, from June 23, to June 25, inclusive----

Brantford, Cases THREE, Deaths 1, Convalescent 2.

(Signed)   SLADE ROBINSON,
Pres't Medical Board.

Hamilton, June 27, 1832.

Cholera travelled from Montreal to Brantford in two weeks.

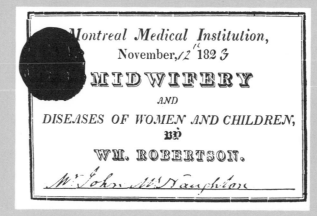

Montreal Medical Institution,
November, 12th 1823
MIDWIFERY
AND
DISEASES OF WOMEN AND CHILDREN,
BY
WM. ROBERTSON.

Mr John McNaughton

Midwives were in great demand since doctors were scarce.

RETURN of cases of Asiatic Cholera admitted into the Emigrant Hospital and Lower Town Hospital, from 8 A. M. on the 23d June, to 8 A. M. on the 24th June, 1832.

	Remaining at last Report.	Admitd since.	Discharged cured.	Convalescent.	Dead.	Remaining.
Emigrant Hospital. -	112	9	6	41	9	106
Lower Town Hospital -	63	7	4	30	7	59
Total	175	16	10	71	16	165
Total of admissions,			674			
Total of deaths,			419			

From the 24th to the 25th:

	Remaining at last report	admitted since	discharged cured	convalescent	dead	remaining
Emigrant Hospital.	106	6	4	42	3	105
Lower Town Hospital.	59	14	6	24	7	60
	165	20	10	66	10	165
Total of admissions,			694			
Total of deaths,			429			

Quebec, 25th June 1832.

T. A. YOUNG,
Secretary Board of Health.

Of every three admitted, two died.

A FORM
OF
PRAYER
WITH
THANKSGIVING,
TO
ALMIGHTY GOD:

TO BE USED UPON SATURDAY, THE 1st DAY OF NOVEMBER, 1834; BEING THE DAY APPOINTED BY PROCLAMATION FOR A GENERAL THANKSGIVING TO ALMIGHTY GOD:

To acknowledge His great Goodness and Mercy in removing from us that grievous Disease, with which several places in these Provinces have been lately visited.

By Authority

KINGSTON, U.C.

PRINTED BY JAMES MACFARLANE AND COMPANY.

1834.

Survivors breathed a prayer of thanks.

was not uncommon – he would run out of food. The ship's crew would then sell him food, at exorbitant prices. A few emigrants literally died of starvation. Others developed scurvy. Water, too, was a problem. Ships were supposed to carry a minimum of fifty-two gallons of water per person, but few owners obeyed this regulation. Sometimes water was stored in casks that had contained indigo, or in one case rancid oil. Sometimes the water was tainted before the ship even set out and when the casks were opened, they were found to be covered with greenish scum.

One pamphlet published by ship-owners to lure Highland Scots aboard claimed that a man would need four stones of oatmeal, and as many of biscuits and butter, four of cutlings for gruel, half a stone of sugar, half a pound of tea, twenty stones of potatoes, and a few dozen eggs. You were supposed to grease the eggs, to keep them fresh. With this diet, only the potatoes would have saved you from scurvy.

what to pack

Advice varied, too, about the other equipment needed. Every commentator agreed that the mahogany furniture should be left behind. Some stressed the necessity of bringing metal clocks, as these were very expensive in the colonies; even a cheap clock with wooden works might cost five pounds. Iron goods and "mangles" might be useful. So would seeds for such crops as clover. Many mentioned shoes and leather goods: these too were expensive in the colonies. Poor emigrants were told to take "only their wearing apparel, with such bedding, or utensils for cooking as may be required on the voyage." But for middle-class emigrants, the list was considerably longer. Ladies were advised to take great care in packing their crystal, china and silver, as well as their bonnets, which were easily crushed. A young single gentle-

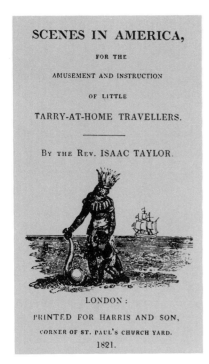

Isaac Taylor's children's book of exploration in Canada took young "tarry-at-home" travellers on wonderful trips with Indians and wild animals. But it wasn't all frivolous! – the book is also for "instruction."

man was advised to bring with him the following "outfit":

I will suppose a young man to have the usual clothes, etc. of a gentleman; in addition to these, let him bring—

A moleskin jacket, price	£ 1 10 0
One doz. striped cotton shirts	2 0 0
One doz. of thick country-knit worsted stockings	1 0 0
Four very warm night caps	0 4 0
Four Guernsey shirts	0 12 0
Four pair flannel drawers	0 14 0
Four blankets	1 10 0
Sailor's jacket, waistcoat and trowsers	2 10 0
Two pair of very strong shoes, high enough to protect the ankle,	1 4 0
Four pillow cases	0 6 0
One curled hair mattress	1 4 0
Six towels	0 5 0
Canteen, with all necessary cooking apparatus	3 10 0
One of Butler's medicine chests, with his medicine directory	2 0 0
One fur cap and gloves	0 15 0
Four pair of thick Russia duck trowsers	1 10 0
One pocket compass	0 3 0
Total,	£20 17 0
With implements and tools amounting to	5 12 0
Total,	£26 9 0

Although a lady in the cabin could get just as sea-sick as a crofter's wife in the steerage, life in the cabin was definitely more enjoyable. Millie and Ellen Steele, two bouncy young ladies from England, made the crossing in 1833 to join their well-to-do father. In the diary which they kept jointly they noted the details of the trip, which they found vastly amusing, especially when the weather was rough. They were always rushing to the windows during storms to admire the waves and the thunder and lightning. If they got drenched, that too was a joke. Dinner was fun, as Ellen commented:

... the Captain was very gallantly handing us up to the table, when a sudden lurch sent a piece of roast pork and a couple of fowls well covered with melted butter rolling at our feet. These were followed by plates, glasses, sauce-boats.... The unfortunate fowls slipped by me two or three times. I really laughed too much to secure them.

the captain's table

Dinner was at four, and while the cabin passengers ate it, the steerage passengers were allowed up on deck. "They are very quiet and orderly," said Ellen, "and as we are in general a decent time at this meal they enjoy it very much." No wonder they were "a decent time" at dinner. They ate and drank very well. William Powell, who crossed in 1834 and kept an equally effervescent journal, describes the meal:

We generally sat down about thirty in number, the capⁿ presiding of course, and during the first part of the voyage we had fresh beef and all the time we were at sea which was about five weeks our mess was furnished with fresh mutton, pork, (both very good) geese, fowls, &c. (bad) salt-beef (not junk) tongues, hams, potatoes, soups, (all very good). These formed the first course. The second consisted of puddings of various sorts, plum, rice and custard, preserved cranberry, gooseberry and cherry tarts. With these and a few glasses of sherry or champagne we managed to get along tolerably well. For dessert we had oranges, almonds and raisins, nuts and hickory nuts, figs and many other little dainties over which and the wine of four or five different kinds, we generally passed away a couple of hours amusing ourselves indifferently well.

In addition to all this, there would be a supper in the evening. If they got seasick, "sago, gruel, arrowroot, lemonade," were served by a steward or stewardess.

When they weren't eating, admiring the waves, sunsets, dolphins and jellyfish, or writing in their journals, the cabin passengers would often have a little music. The Steeles' ship had a piano, two violins and three flutes. The gentlemen sang glees. When they were tired of this, they "ran after each other up and down the ladders and ropes." Ellen Steele thought this a rather dangerous amusement. Sometimes, during a storm, the gentlemen would further entertain themselves by playing upon the fears of the ladies, telling them the ship had sprung a leak, the long-boat had washed overboard, "and many more of the same description. It was certes very ungallant," says William Powell, "but we could not help having a little fun."

But rich or poor, cabin or steerage, there were some dangers emigrants had in common. If the steerage had cholera, the cabin was threatened. If the ship sank, all would drown. And all alike were subject to theft. Books for emigrants repeatedly warned against this. Even potatoes should be kept in barrels with locks. All property should be plainly marked. "Have nothing in bags," said one authority. "I would warn you to look sharp, for sailors and passengers will sometimes make mistakes as to what is their own and what is not."

a cargo of Plaster of Paris

When the ship finally reached land, the troubles of the emigrants were not over. The usual dumping grounds for poor emigrants were Halifax and Pictou in Nova Scotia, or Quebec City, but if a ship had been a long time on the voyage and food was low, an unscrupulous captain might simply land the emigrants anywhere at all. One such ship, crowded with starving passengers, finally reached the north shore of the Saint Lawrence. Here the captain made the passengers get off. They were stranded on an unknown coast, with no town or village in sight and no provisions. A pass-

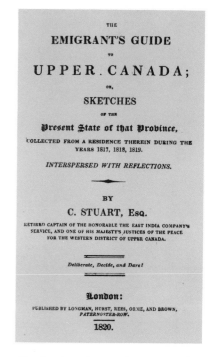

THE

EMIGRANT'S GUIDE

TO

UPPER CANADA;

OR,

SKETCHES

OF THE

Present State of that Province,

COLLECTED FROM A RESIDENCE THEREIN DURING THE
YEARS 1817, 1818, 1819.

INTERSPERSED WITH REFLECTIONS.

BY

C. STUART, ESQ.

RETIRED CAPTAIN OF THE HONORABLE THE EAST INDIA COMPANY'S
SERVICE, AND ONE OF HIS MAJESTY'S JUSTICES OF THE PEACE
FOR THE WESTERN DISTRICT OF UPPER CANADA.

Deliberate, Decide, and Dare!

London:

PUBLISHED BY LONGMAN, HURST, REES, ORME, AND BROWN,
PATERNOSTER-ROW.
1820.

Charles Stuart's moralizing guide for emigrants—one of dozens written in the period—emphasized that there were many opportunities in Upper Canada for the "industrious poor" to work hard and improve their lives.

These statistics were noted in an 1839 history of Montreal, which called Asiatic Cholera "the most fearful form of pestilence in modern times. In Montreal the epidemic brought all business to a standstill, kept visitors away and put many residents to flight.

One look at the interior of a packet shows that the upper classes could be just as vulnerable to seasickness as were steerage passengers. Basins were kept close for use on short notice.

ing ship took pity on them and picked them up, but it was carrying a cargo of Plaster of Paris. The ship ran into a storm, the overloaded ship took in water, the Plaster of Paris got wet, and the ship sank. All the emigrants were drowned.

If they did manage to reach Halifax, Pictou, or Quebec the emigrants found no warm welcome. There were not enough facilities to accommodate the hordes that were arriving, and the inhabitants were often hostile. Even if the ship had made the voyage without disease, it might find a plague raging in the city, brought by some previous ship. The emigrants would step from the steerage only to find themselves in something worse–the quarantine sheds, where the sick and the dead lay heaped together, and, again, the food was scarce and the water bad. Susanna Moodie remarked that these sheds "greatly resembled cattle pens."

At Quebec, during the cholera plague of 1832, passengers were required to land at Grosse Isle for "purification." (Cabin passengers did not have to get purified in person: they could send a servant with the bedding.) The emigrants were supposed to wash themselves, their clothing and their bedding in the river. Men and boys, jubilant after their long confinement, leapt into the river; women tucked up their skirts and tramped their bedding "in tubs or in holes in the rocks." Mrs. Moodie could not understand why the people were behaving in such an uproarious way, running around half-naked, "insolent and noisy," "singing, drinking, dancing, shouting, and cutting antics that would surprise the leader of a circus." Perhaps if she had just spent seven weeks in the steerage she would have understood.

If Britain had not been the Garden of Eden, neither were the colonies. Still, they were not a total desert either, and, for a poor man, they offered one thing which Europe could no longer offer: hope. Those who had survived the crossing, the disease, the hunger and the human jackals, had something to look forward to.

" 'Whurrah! my boys,' " Mrs. Moodie heard an Irishman shouting, " 'Shure we'll all be jintlemen!' " The promised land, or the land where land was promised, had been reached.

THE EMIGRANTS WELCOME TO CANADA.

London Pub. by O. Hodgson 10 Cloth Fair

This far-fetched cartoon lampoons the middle-class emigrants who went to the Canadas loaded down with trappings of their genteel life, unprepared for the new country and new challenges. Many of these people got rude shocks when trying to set up farming estates in the bush and decided to settle in the villages instead.

The New Land

For most settlers in colonial Canada, their new land meant acres for crops. Scottish crofters, English farm labourers and Irish potato growers, without a hope of owning land at home, could become masters of their own destiny in the colonies, provided they worked hard enough. First they had to spend months cutting brush, felling trees, tugging at stumps and lugging rocks off the heavily forested land. Only then could they plant.

John A. Macdonald walked three miles to school from this house in Hay Bay, near Adolphustown, in U.C. His father, Hugh, had bad luck as a shopkeeper and miller in various settlements, but the family scraped together the money for John's schooling. "Ye'll hear something from Johnny yet," was Hugh's prediction.

Not only farms had to be carved out of the wilderness: townsites as well were originally no more than dense forest. Here woodsmen's axes clear the way for the town of Stanley, N.B.

Hay for your horse was included on the room bill at the Stanley, N.B. tavern. The town was founded by a land company which was later crippled by incompetent officials.

Thomas Fead's painting shows a group of Scottish emigrants passing Sunday in the backwoods. The Bible is the centre of attention, at least for the older folks.

CHAPTER THREE

The Young Emigrants

I assure you there cannot well be a more un-poetical and anti-romantic existence than ours.

Anne Langton, *A Gentlewoman in Upper Canada,* 1839

In 1826, six years before she actually went to Canada, Catherine Parr Traill published a children's book called *The Young Emigrants; or, Pictures of Canada.* According to the title page, the author hoped that it would "inculcate. . . the lessons of mental firmness, piety, and industry."

The book tells the story of the Clarence family, whose father, a gentleman of modest means, is thrown out of work by government cutbacks, a common enough plight in the postwar recession. Rather than go into trade and descend into "the lower ranks of society," the family decides to use the money from the sale of their small estate, "Roselands," to emigrate to Upper Canada. None of the Clarences really wants to do this. Sister Ellen is the most strongly opposed: " 'I have always conceived such a great dislike to the character of the Americans,' " she sighs, " 'that I cannot endure the idea of living among them.' " But the other two children, Richard and Agnes, determine to do their duty. Fifteen-year-old Richard sells some of his "amusing instruments connected with science," namely, "a small electrifying machine, an air-pump, a cabinet of fossils, and a superb magic lantern." With the money so obtained, he

goes to a local carpenter, learns a little carpentry, and purchases some tools. He then spends a few weeks with a farmer, and Agnes accompanies him to learn about poultry and dairies. Her mother approves. " 'Why,' " said she, " 'should these offices be unbecoming to a lady, merely because they are useful?' "

Richard realizes that life in the colonies will of necessity be practical; yet his overall view is romantic. Both he and his father consider agriculture preferable to, for instance, being a grocer: "What can be a more manly and independent employment, than that which God first ordained for man?. . . At any rate, it is more consonant to our habits, than engaging in any mercantile pursuits." His father warns him he will have to give up luxuries, but Richard's reply is enthusiastic: " 'And will not the fire burn as brightly, if made with wood and kindled on a hearth, as in this highly-polished stove?. . . and will not wooden stools, and couches with fur cushions, be as comfortable as these gilded chairs and sofas? and rush matting, with a bear's skin rug, be as warm to our feet as this gay carpet?' " His sisters, however, weep at such a prospect: " 'In America,' " Ellen wails, " 'what will be the use of those accomplishments, that Agnes and I have spent so much time in attaining?' " Richard cheers her up: " 'My dear sister. . . if you see things in their right light, you will perceive that your French will be useful to you in conversing with the

The frontispiece of Catherine Parr Traill's The Young Emigrants.

Young Macalister seems sad at the prospect of leaving Scotland for British North America. Many emigrants from Great Britain used the colonies as a jumping-off point, and ended up in the States.

Canadians, who speak that language. Music will cheer our evenings, after the toils of the day; and as to drawing, remember, Ellen, how many beautiful flowers Canada produces, which will form new and interesting studies for your pencil. ' "

The anxieties and reactions of the Clarences illuminate those of a whole class of British emigrants – the impoverished gentlefolk, those younger sons of good families, half-pay officers and minor officials whose sinecures had become obsolete. The fear uppermost in their minds was that by going to the Canadas and dipping their hands in the soil, they would lose class. Their foremost hope was that they would be able to recoup their fallen fortunes and gain a social position equal to the one they felt by rights to be theirs. Visions of landed gentry danced in their heads. But few were Richard Clarences or even sensible Catherine Parr Traills. Most were like Richard's accomplished but helpless sister Ellen, or Catherine's equally accomplished and equally helpless sister, Susanna Moodie.

cheats and profiteers

In the late twenties and thirties, such people poured into British North America by the thousands. As Susanna Moodie said, "Canada became the great landmark for the rich in hope and poor in purse." These gentlefolk were lured by the prevailing "Canadamania," by the blandishments of unscrupulous land-agents who held meetings and hired orators to address them, and by "pamphlets, published by interested parties, which prominently set forth all the *good* to be derived from a settlement in the Backwoods of Canada," but neglected to mention any of the ills. These people were naive, ignorant of the perils awaiting them, unused to physical labour, class-conscious and proud. Thus they were natural targets for cheats and profiteers, and many of them failed miserably. Their worst fears were realized; according to Moodie, the sons of poor gentlemen "generally lost caste and sunk into useless sots," while those of the lower classes, more used to privation and toil, were able to rise above them.

Mrs. Traill based *The Young Emigrants* on two early travel books and some letters from a friend, all of which were fairly sanguine about life in the colonies. She and her sister must have looked back on this little children's book with a certain irony when they themselves encountered the real thing. The Clarences were too good to be true, but the experiences of the gentle settlers must have seemed at times too bad to be believed.

it all seemed so easy

From a distance it all seemed so easy. First you had to make the crossing, which was admittedly a danger; but of course the genteel emigrant would spend extra money for a cabin rather than a steerage passage. The fictional Clarences found the trip rather delightful, and behaved with "great firmness" during the storms. Catherine Parr Traill also behaved with great firmness, though her complaint was seasickness. Her cabin, with its crimson draperies and handsome sofa, cost fifteen pounds a head, but the Traills felt they had no choice, since the only other ship available at the time was "literally swarming with emigrants, chiefly of the lower class of Highlanders."

Once in the colonies, according to *The Young Emigrants,* all you had to do was locate your land-grant, if you had one, or purchase a farm if you didn't. Then, once you had reached your land, you settled in. If the land was partially cleared, with buildings already on it, your task was simple. You would put in a crop, clear more land and convert the trees to potash or timber, start increasing your livestock, and, like Mr. Clarence, make "English improvements," such as corn stands, five-barred

gates, hay stacks and sheep pens, which would "astonish the neighbours." Needless to say, your work would be mainly supervisory; there would be hired hands to do the actual physical labour. The ladies of the family, when not sketching wild flowers and conversing in French with the natives, might turn their hands to dairying, planting rosebushes, baking, and feeding the calves and poultry; they too, naturally, would have servants to help them. In the winters everyone would have fun sleighing and skating, and the evenings would pass in "social chat or innocent gaity," with the family and equally genteel neighbours gathered round the blazing hearth, singing, playing the flute, reading aloud, drawing, or playing chess or backgammon. The land would be fertile and the weather something like England's, though with hotter summers and snowier winters.

buying a farm

In reality, the middle-class English emigrants were more likely to astonish the neighbours by their ignorance and gullibility than by their improvements. Many were the ex-army officers who transported their families across the Atlantic only to find that their grants were not in the fertile, flat and balmy Niagara region but in a swamp, on a rocky hillside or on a ridge of sand. The early arrivals who had enticed the others over with their glowing reports had already taken the really good land. Then, too, even the seemingly fertile soil was quickly depleted, and unless you had the foresight to manure it, your farm would soon be exhausted.

The fictional Clarences buy their farm from a friendly and honest Montreal land-agent, quite different from the "artful seducers" and "rogues" the Moodies encountered. For a mere five hundred pounds, they get eight hundred acres of uncleared land and a hundred and fifty cleared, with a "log-house, a barn, a root-house, stable, hen-house and

**Samuel Strickland
A Land Agent**

To Samuel Strickland emigration was a "wholesome channel through which the superfluous population of England and Ireland passes from a state of poverty to one of comfort." It was a good definition, even enticing for those few who had the education to understand it and the money to afford the cabin fare to make the voyage to Upper Canada. Strickland himself came to Canada in 1825 at age 21 — seven years before his sisters — as a land agent for the Canada Company. Like most other well-bred emigrants, he joined the militia where he served during the days of rebellion. He was the father of 14 children by three marriages, and despite his various government commissions, he knew the settler's hardships — his own, his sisters' and his clients'. His memoir, *Twenty-seven Years in Canada West,* is a graphic account of his experience.

pig-stye." They don't like the log house, which only has five rooms, with miserable seven-foot ceilings, in addition to the kitchen, store-room, root-cellar and ice-house. So they immediately demolish it and build a frame house. They plan this house in a day, then hold a bee, and in three days their house is up. Richard astounds the locals with his knowledge of "the art of dove-tail and morticing." He also comments on the bee: "You have seen a hive of bees or a nest of ants. . . all united in labouring for the common good. . . . I think you would have been amused by the ant-like industry and public spirit evinced by our kind neighbours." Their new house has a parlour, a study, a kitchen, a storeroom, a back kitchen, a porch, and a dairy, with four bedrooms upstairs and a loft for the servants. Mrs. Clarence finds the black pipes of iron heating stoves ugly, so their parlour is heated by a fireplace. In the kitchen they have an oven and a flat hearth of stone over which cooking pots can be suspended.

a leaky one-room shack

This house, which the Clarences consider rather rustic, was an undreamed-of luxury for most settlers. Such a house could not be built without proximity to a saw-mill, and most settlements were so remote and the roads so bad that even a door made of saw-mill planks was a rarity. Even the despised five-room log house was splendid compared with most. More usual was the Moodies' first place, a rented house described to them, sight unseen, as "a delightful summer residence," which turned out to be a doorless, leaky, one-room shack. "You must be mistaken," Mrs. Moodie said to the driver. "That is not a house, but a cattle-shed or pig-stye." Such houses were made of squared logs notched at the ends and chinked with moss or bark, covered perhaps with clay (which, Anne Langton noted, was both-

ersome as it was always falling out). Wallpaper was out of the question, but sometimes the logs were whitewashed to make them look cleaner. The roof was probably of halved and hollowed-out basswood logs overlapping each other, or of four-foot-long cedar-bark shingles. The floor was of beaten earth or of halved logs with the flat side up. Newly-built shanties were not surrounded by the picturesque shade-trees of the Clarences, but by mud and charred stumps. Settlers considered trees their enemies, especially around a house where they could spread flies. These shacks, even when festooned with hop vines as Mrs. Traill recommended, looked bleak, crude and mean to genteel people newly arrived from England.

furnishing her new house

The Traills had a better log house, with three upstairs bedrooms, which they raised by holding a bee. These affairs were not the jolly altruistic events pictured by Richard Clarence. According to Mrs. Moodie, they were "noisy, riotous, drunken meetings, often terminating in violent quarrels, sometimes even in bloodshed." She felt the money expended on food and drink would have been better spent on hired labourers. Mrs. Traill, who usually had better luck than her sister, invited sixteen men, and served them plenty of "Canadian nectar (whisky)," some joints of salt pork, a peck of potatoes, rice pudding, and "a loaf as big as an enormous Cheshire cheese."

Mrs. Traill furnished her new house with a "handsome Franklin stove, with brass gallery and fender," a brass-railed sofa, "Canadian painted chairs," a pine table, muslin curtains, and an "Indian mat." She hung maps and prints on the walls, and – unlike more primitive settlers – had a wallfull of books as well. "Our bedchamber," she said, "is furnished with equal simplicity." She doesn't describe the bed, but it was probably a

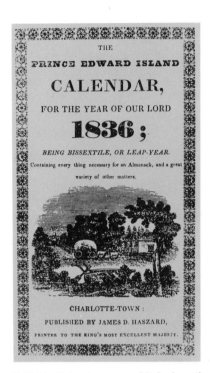

THE
PRINCE EDWARD ISLAND
CALENDAR,
FOR THE YEAR OF OUR LORD
1836;
BEING BISSEXTILE, OR LEAP-YEAR.
Containing every thing necessary for an Almanack, and a great variety of other matters.

CHARLOTTE-TOWN:
PUBLISHED BY JAMES D. HASZARD,
PRINTER TO THE KING'S MOST EXCELLENT MAJESTY.

P.E.I.'s Calendar was published until 1873, and is thought to be the first on the island. Early Canadian almanacks contained information on agriculture, literature, the law, and bits of invaluable homespun philosophy.

four-poster with a straw or feather tick. Straw ticks, with an opening in the middle of the top side so the housewife could reach in and redistribute the straw, were used before enough chicken, duck or goose feathers could be saved from the poultry for a feather one. The Traills may have had a counterpane brought from England; or they may have had a bedcover or homespun, or a patchwork quilt. Linen sheets were hard to come by. The Traills probably had a warming-pan, but those without used hot bricks or stones on cold winter nights.

The Moodies' first shack had one window, with only one pane of glass in it. Windows with real glass were a luxury, unless you were near a store that sold the panes, and so were the iron heating stoves Mrs. Clarence found so disagreeable. Cooking was done on a single rough fireplace, sometimes just a flat stone and a hole in the roof. If you were lucky and had money and access to a stonemason, you might have a real mantelpiece and a stone chimney, but more likely you would only have a firebacking of fieldstones cemented with clay and a chimney made of clay-covered wickerwork. These fireplaces were dirty and hot to cook over, and if the wind was in the wrong direction or the house drafty, they would fill the house with smoke. There was no shortage of firewood; but someone had to cut it down, chop it up and lug it to the house.

salt pork, potatoes and bread

The imaginary Clarences have a separate kitchen. They also have a variety of things to cook in it. Their livestock consists of oxen, cows, sheep, pigs, geese, chickens, ducks and pigeons, and they grow fruit trees and a variety of vegetables. They bake bread, cakes, puddings and pastry, and preserve fruit with maple syrup, which they hire the Indians to make. They make butter and cheese,

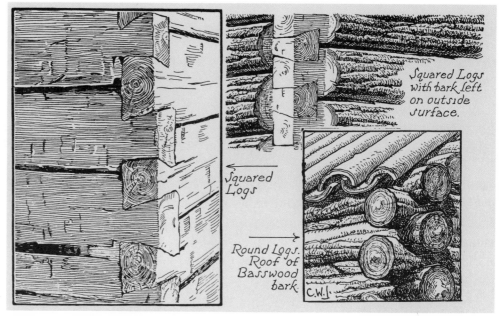

Building a Log Cabin

The only requirements for a log cabin were a trusty axe, a nearby forest to swing it at, a knowledge of notching, and a crew of robust neighbours to help fit the pieces together. A pail of whisky helped keep the workers working, even if it cost them a toe or two.

Cooking Utensils

Log cabin cooking was done over an open hearth, with a limited number of iron and copper utensils. A kitchen might have only a spit, a boiler, long and short-handled frying pans, ladles, skimmers, a tea kettle and a bake-kettle, but these were enough in good hands. With bread dough in the bake kettle covered with hot coals, meat on the spit, corn-on-the-cob in the boiler, and a tea kettle steaming, dinner need not have disappointed anybody. The importance of knowing how to use these tools was detailed in the dozens of "Guides to Emigrants" that were printed.

Meat Chopper

Gravy Strainer

Beefsteak Tongs

Bachelor's Frying Pan

2-Gallon Boiling Pot

Sauté Pan

Reflector Oven with Vertical Spit and Jack

Fish Frier

Toaster and Trivet

Dripping-pan and Ladle

and they have a flower garden.

The truth was that until a farm was well established, the staple foods were salt pork, potatoes and bread, if you had any flour. Even if you grew wheat, it was hard to get it ground unless you were near a grist mill. Corn meal was often substituted. If you wanted maple syrup and sugar, you had to make it yourself, and the backbreaking all-night operation of boiling down the sap and sugaring-off was performed by the women and children. Poultry was likely to die on the Atlantic voyage, and cows too were sickly and scarce. Even for those fortunate enough to have their own cow, butter-making in a wooden dasher churn was a crude and lengthy process, and the cellar where the butter had to be stored was often a mouldy-smelling hole in the ground.

"The black bread of Sparta"

The Clarences had an oven built right into their kitchen fireplace, but this too was a luxury. Most women baked in a "bake-kettle," a heavy iron pot with a lid, like a Dutch oven. The bread was put into the bake-kettle and the whole thing was covered with coals and ashes. If you didn't know how to do this, or how to make your own yeast out of "milk-emptyings," or how to make salt-rising sponge, you would end up with a flat loaf burned to a crisp, like poor Mrs. Moodie's. "The black bread of Sparta," her friend Tom Wilson quipped, as he stuck his knife through the charred crust and brought it out covered with raw dough.

Baking in a bake-kettle wasn't the only thing Mrs. Moodie didn't know how to do. Although she was not from a rich family, she, like everyone of her class, had taken servants for granted. The Clarences overcame the Canadian servant shortage by rescuing a whole family of Highland Scots from disease and starvation, but the Moodies did not have the foresight to do this. Their servants were always demanding to eat at the same table with them or deserting at crucial moments, leaving Mrs. Moodie to face some frightening task on her own. She was so terrified the first time she had to milk a cow that she ran over to a neighbour's to ask for help. She had never done a washing before she came to Canada and, the first time she attempted to heat water for one, she almost smoked herself and her family out of the house. She didn't know how to dry apples, so lost her whole crop to an old woman who offered to do it for her and then stole the results. A good settler's wife made her own soap, raised her own sheep and dyed and spun the wool, and made her own candles from animal fat rendered after the fall slaughtering. Home-making was literally that: everything in the home was made. Mrs. Moodie did not know how to do any of these things and had to spend precious money for items like candles and soap.

the domestic arts

After seven years in the bush, she had mastered some of these domestic arts; she could make coffee from dandelion roots, for instance. But a wife of a lower class would have been expected to do much more. Agnes Clarence's claim that her labours were "light" would have been greeted with a rude laugh by most settlers' wives. In addition to the cooking, kitchen-gardening, butchering and meat-curing, spinning, sugar-making, dairy and poultry work, rule-of-thumb doctoring and midwifery, and child-raising, she would have helped the men with the crops—potatoes before the stumps of the cut trees had been hauled out of the ground, wheat when the land was fit for a plough. She would bind sheaves of cut wheat, help with fences (brush, root or, if you had pretensions, split rail), and, if necessary, plough, chop, and do any other man's work that needed to be done.

The Maple Tree
A Canadian Song

When the snows of winter are melting fast,
   And the sap begins to rise,
And the biting breath of the frozen blast
   Yields to the Spring's soft sighs,
     Then away to the wood,
     For the maple, good,
Shall unlock its honied store;
   And boys and girls,
   With their sunny curls,
     Bring their vessels brimming o'er
      With the luscious flood
      Of the brave tree's blood,
Into cauldrons deep to pour.

The blaze from the sugar-bush gleams red;
   Far down in the forest dark,
A ruddy glow on the tree is shed,
   That lights up the rugged bark;
     And with merry shout,
     The busy rout
Watch the sap as it bubbles high;
   And they talk of the cheer
Of the coming year,
     And the jest and the song pass by;
     And brave tales of old
     Round the fire are told,
That kindle youth's beaming eye.

Susanna Moodie's maple sugar song catches the festive atmosphere of tapping the sap—"the brave tree's blood"—in pioneer days.

Portable Soup

PUT on, in four gallons of water, ten pounds of a shin of beef, free from fat and skin, six pounds of a knuckle of veal, and two fowls; break the bones and cut the meat into small pieces; season with one ounce of whole black pepper, quarter of an ounce of Jamaica pepper, and the same of mace; cover the pot very closely, and let it simmer twelve or fourteen hours, and then strain it. The following day take off the fat and clear the jelly from any sediment adhering to it; boil it gently upon a stove without covering the sauce-pan, and stir it frequently till it thickens to a strong glue. Pour it into broad tin pans, and put in a cool oven. When it will take the impression of a knife, score it in equal squares. Stand it in a south window or near a stove. When dry, break it at the scores. Wrap it in paper, and put it closely up in boxes. There should always be a large supply of this soup, as with it and catsup no one will ever be at a loss for dressed dishes and soups.

Instant soup—pioneer style—came in four-gallon batches, according to this hearty recipe. For the best results, use a pipkin (earthen pot).

One of the worst chores she had was potash-boiling, but as potash was likely to be a farmer's first cash "crop," it was an important one. The men girdled the hardwood trees, acres of them at a time, burned them in piles and leached the lye out of the ashes by pouring water over them. The women boiled the residue, stirring it with a ten-foot ladle until it was dark red. It took a week to make one barrel of potash which sold in Montreal for thirty dollars, and for the last few days the boiling lye had to be stirred incessantly. English gentlewomen were simply incapable of such feats, and their husbands' farms often failed because they lacked the supply of unpaid female labour necessary to turn a profit.

And if you did fail, many of the neighbours would cheer. The Moodies were unprepared for the malice and vindictiveness of the Yankee squatters or working-class British emigrants around them, who regarded the genteel English as fools and dupes and greatly resented their old-country customs and assumptions of superiority. In Traill's book, the Clarences find neighbours of their own class, helpful, courteous and kind, and the local farmers voluntarily plough up the Clarences' fields for them, lend them seed, and even sow it for them. The Moodies, on the other hand, were bedevilled by their neighbours, who tricked them, sneered at them, and borrowed everything the Moodies were stupid enough to lend them: sugar, tea, thread, clothing, combs, candles, flour. When they moved from their first shack into a bigger log house, they found that the vacating tenants had girdled all the orchard trees, flooded their floor and hidden a dead skunk in their mantelpiece. In later years, Mrs. Moodie tried hard to understand the motivations for such acts, and she realized that the English class system was repressive.

The Clarences name their Canadian house "Roselands," after the English home they left. Their dream is the re-creation of England on Canadian soil, but it was a dream that could never be realized outside the pages of a children's fairy-tale. Even in *The Young Emigrants,* there are some curiously prophetic omissions. For instance, we are told all about Agnes and Richard, but once they hit Canadian soil, Mrs. Clarence, except for her objection to the stovepipes, fades from view. Perhaps only the young could adapt themselves to a life so very different from the one they had known. Or perhaps Mrs. Clarence was a victim of the melancholy and depression so often noticed among Canadian wives, especially those from the educated classes. Even when a family had, by hard work and real privation, established something like the Clarence dream home, the women repined. Men could get out of the house, to hunt and fish or go to the local tavern, but women were stuck in their isolated houses, looking at four walls and a lot of stumps and trees. The amazing thing is not that so many of these genteel settlers folded up, but that so many made it through.

Susanna Moodie named her first daughter "Agnes." Perhaps this was a family name. It would be touching to think, however, that she may have named her after the imaginary Agnes Clarence, in the hope that her daughter would be more suited to the new world than she herself had been.

Pioneer Women

Anne Langton

Anne Langton was educated in Rome and Switzerland; yet this gentlewoman spent her days as a spinster on her brother's farm near Sturgeon Lake, U.C. She endured the many hardships of life in the not-quite tamed wilds, and in her journal, *A Gentlewoman in Upper Canada,* wrote: "I assure you there cannot well be a more unpoetical and unromantic existence than ours." For all her schooling, she could not have been prepared for the toils and trials of butchering cattle, making candles and soap, baking and withstanding the unrelenting cold of winter. As was the pattern in the early homesteads, once the farm was running smoothly, there was time for other interests. Ann taught children in the district, wrote journals and painted sketches of rural life. But Anne Langton and the Sturgeon Lake community were unusual in 1835: four were university graduates.

Susanna Moodie

"My love for Canada was a feeling very nearly allied to that which the condemned criminal entertains for his cell." Susanna Moodie was a long time forgetting her upper-class birth and rearing. She first settled near Cobourg, U.C., in 1832 with her husband, John Moodie. She was 29 years old then. Two years later the Moodies moved north to a 400-acre homestead near Peterborough, to be nearer her brother and sister, Catherine Parr Traill. For all her grumbling about pioneer life, discomfort and endless toil, and her haughty disdain for lower-class customs and crudeness, she was an often witty and colourful chronicler of everyday life in the period. She published many stories, poems and sketches in *The Literary Garland* and *Victoria Magazine* but is best known for her candid book, *Roughing It in the Bush* (1852).

Catherine Parr Traill

There was a cholera epidemic raging when Catherine Parr Traill landed at Grosse Isle in 1832. Unlike the hundreds of steerage passengers who had contracted the disease and were left to die at the quarantine station, her husband removed her immediately to Montreal and proper medical care. Their destination was her brother's farm in Upper Canada, and in September the Traills joined the Stricklands. Unlike her hard-luck sister, Susanna, Catherine approached the hardships of pioneer life with practical sense, strength and optimism. She accepted the backwoods isolation and hardships far better than any of the other women whose writings have survived, and her *Female Emigrant's Guide* (1852) quickly became an indispensable and best-selling handbook. Despite debt and disasters, she wrote a dozen more books and died at the age of 97.

Anna Jameson

Anna Brownell Murphy was strong-minded, independent, outspoken. In 1825, at age 31, she became Mrs. Robert Jameson, but when he was sent to Dominica, she stayed in England. When he became attorney general of Upper Canada in 1833, Anna waited three years before joining him. She stayed only eight months, they agreed to separate and she returned home, but not before a whirlwind tour of the province. At Niagara Falls she was "speechless with disappointment." She had hated Toronto — "a fourth-or fifth-rate provincial city" — but her spirits lifted when she toured the rugged west of U.C. In one of her books, *Winter Studies and Summer Rambles in Canada,* she describes with wit, precision and enthusiasm the backwoods life. But she confessed she never met "so many repining and discontented women as in Canada," and left before she became one.

To Everything a Season

Apart from newspapers, almanacks were the only written entertainment to cross many early Canadian thresholds. Few readers minded the irregular spelling and grammar, and mangled dialect was part of the fun. Cartoons had political edges, social commentary came with a bite, and home remedies abounded. And in the long winter nights one could ponder "Idleness is the great prodigality," or some other proverb crammed into the almanack's busy pages.

1836]   **APRIL, XXX Days.**   [7

The end of learning, is to know God, and out of that knowledge to love him and to imitate him, as we may the nearest, by possessing our souls of true virtue.

A good conscience is to the soul what health is to the body.
A danger foreseen is half avoided.

8]   **MAY, XXXI Days.**   [1836

Without mounting by degrees, a man cannot attain to high things.
A mind well trained and long exercised in virtue, does not early change any course it once undertakes.

Idleness is the greatest prodigality.
Poverty wants some, luxury many, avarice all things.

12]   **SEPTEMBER, XXX Days.**   [1836

The friends thou hast and their adoption tried,
Grapple them to thy soul with hooks of steel;
But do not dull thy palm with entertainment

Of each new hatched, unfledged comrade.
Thrice is he armed that hath his quarrel just.

1836]   **OCTOBER, XXXI Days.**   [13

It is shameful for a man to live in his own country and to be uninformed of its affairs and interests.
Industry is fortune's right hand; frugality her left.

An uncultivated mind, like unmanured ground, will soon be overrun with weeds.

A COUNTRY *GRUB* CHANGED TO A CITY *BUTTERFLY.*

This is a portrait of a raw and unsophisticated child of nature, leaving his hoe and rake to become a tape and needle clerk, and ends by becoming a *rake* himself.

A caterpillar no more, the butterfly shines forth the effects of two years' counterjumping in the city : " I say, Jem, say, me ; and if it was'nt for lary's cursed low, demsour krout, I could'nt go March Street."

A RADICAL GRIND-STONE,

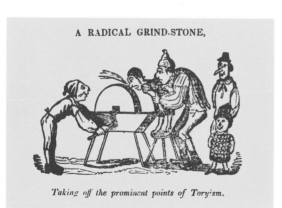

Taking off the prominent points of Toryism.

YANKEE LIBERTY.

The following advertisement is taken from the Delaware Gazette :

FOR SALE—A Negro man, aged about 24 years, he is stout and healthy, accustomed to hard work.   Enquire of G. HOUSTON.

A FITTING PAIR.

" Sure such a pair was never seen,
By nature formed to come together."

NATIVES OF THE *SILLY ISLES,*
Or, *Marks of Intelligence.*

" What are you jumping after there ?" said a schoolmaster to an urchin who stood up to his eyes in shirt collar.

" I wanted to spit, sir," was the reply, " and I was jumping up to try to spit over my dickey."

Praise without profit, puts little in the pocket.

Seek till you find, and you will not lose your labour.

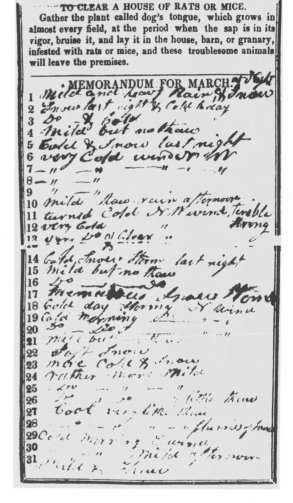

Ships of the Hudson's Bay Company, the Prince of Wales *and the* Eddystone, *are shown bartering with Eskimos of the Upper Savage Islands in 1819.*

CHAPTER FOUR

The Beaver Club

It has been found that Colonisation is at all times unfavourable to the fur trade.

Alexander Mackenzie, of the North West Company, 1811

It was late in a February evening in 1817, at the height of the winter social season in Montreal. The waiter at the Mansion House Hotel, hurrying towards the closed doors of the "elegant suite of Ball and Supper Rooms" with yet another bottle of brandy, three more of port, and several glasses to replace those already broken, could hear a rumble of male voices, interspersed with table-poundings, foot-thumpings and the occasional shout. It was the fortnightly meeting of the Beaver Club, and the members were quite literally whooping it up. They had already gone through part of their club ritual. They had eaten their pemmican, imported especially from the West; they had drunk their prescribed toasts, which included "Voyageurs, Wives and Children" and "Absent Members." They were doubtless preparing for the ceremony of *Le Grand Voyage*, for which they would seize the poker, the fire-tongs, their walking-sticks or swords and, swinging their implements as paddles, would sing the songs of the voyageurs which they had learned during many a long journey. Few of them would have actually had to paddle, and at portages they would have been carried to and from the shore through the icy water on the backs of the voyageurs. Still, they had been there. Soon, the waiter knew, there would be an interval of wild and unmelodious wailing. Later it would be his job to assist the gentlemen who remained in the room to their feet, after which he would have to sweep up the shattered glass and dispose of the furniture that had come apart during a graphic demonstration of rapids-shooting, done off the dining table with an empty wine keg as a canoe.

The management of the exclusive Mansion House Hotel did not mind the noise or the damage. Everything would be handsomely paid for, they knew, and it was an honour to have one's wine glasses smashed in the service of the Beaver Club. For the Beaver Club was no ordinary club. It had already been in existence for thirty-two years, it was the first of its kind in the Provinces, and it was the cultural expression of the North West Company, that band of adventurers which rivalled the Hudson's Bay Company in power and which had kept Montreal as important as London in the fur trade. Membership in it was limited and select: only fifty-five could belong at a time, new members being added as old ones died, and no one could join who had not "wintered over" in the vast western territories.

The only outward badge of membership was the small gold medallion each wore suspended from a blue ribbon. "Beaver Club," the medallion read, or (for the Club was bilingual) "Coterie du

Members of the Beaver Club wore a gold medallion on a blue ribbon at club affairs. Only those few who had "wintered over" were eligible to join

Castor." In the centre of the medal was a beaver gnawing at a tree, with the slogan "Industry and Perseverance" and the date of the member's first winter in the field. The medallions were all individually engraved, some not too skilfully; a few of the beavers looked like armadillos, others like dogs, seals or tigers. On the obverse was the member's name, the slogan "Fortitude In Distress," and an engraving of four men in a canoe, with hats balanced on the tops of their heads like stove-lids, teetering on the edge of something that was supposed to be a rapids but looked more like a waterfall.

Fur trading voyageurs gathered at the Montreal waterfront with the long winter's booty. For almost two centuries their take formed the economic foundation of the city's money and banking.

women's work in the fur trade

The slogans, the songs, the badges, the flags and the rituals were not mere ornaments, tacked on to a mundane counting-house business. They were true expressions of the emotions these men felt towards the Company, which in almost all respects was more like a feudal society than a modern commercial enterprise. The Company had been formed largely by Highland Scots, with their clan loyalties and traditions and the bitter memory of Culloden still fresh in their memories. They had taken over a system begun by the French, which had been equally feudal. The Company demanded from all of its members, partners and employees alike, the most unwavering devotion and obedience. Any deviation was regarded as treachery, almost like the betrayal of a Chief. But long service and loyalty were rewarded. The Company took care of its own.

The fur trade as practised by the North West Company was composed of several interlocking hierarchies, each dependent upon the other. At the very bottom, of course, were the animals whose skins were peeled off to cover the backs and heads of rich and fashionable Europeans. They had little to say in the matter and received none of the pro-

fits. Next came the Indians, many of whom had become totally dependent on the fur trade. The Indian men did the trapping of fur animals and the shooting of buffalo with traps and guns acquired by trade from the Company. But it was on the back-breaking labour of the Indian and Métis women that the survival of the trade depended. Not only did they dress the hides, sew the moccasins used by Indian and voyageur alike, and net the snowshoes, they also acted as porters when no dogs or horses were available. The Indian man, unlike the voyageur, did not consider it a manly feat to carry two or three ninety-pound packs across a portage. Carrying bundles was women's work. So was gathering the repair materials for canoes, and skinning and gutting the buffalo, and so was the hard labour of pounding the meat into pemmican with stone mallets. Ten buffalo could be killed as easily as one by an Indian with a gun, but it took an Indian woman ten times as long to turn them into pemmican. Before the fur trade, the women had to make winter supplies only for their own people. Now, pemmican was a trade item, and, as it was the only food both portable enough and nourishing enough to feed the voyageurs on their long non-stop trips between Fort William and Montreal, they had to make large amounts of it. One voyageur alone needed to eat several pounds of pemmican a day.

syphilis and smallpox

What did the Indian women get in return for their labour? Sometimes they got syphilis or smallpox. They got copper pots instead of birchbark ones, and they got cheap cotton and blanket cloth. They got needles and thread and the pleasure of sewing the coloured trade beads – "mock coral," "barley corn," "mock garnet," "enamelled," "blue agate," and the many more listed in the Company's inventories – into beautiful patterns for their men's clothes. They also got acknowledgement of a kind: the Company knew their importance, as it knew the importance of the beaver and buffalo. And it valued them as "wives."

axes, tobacco and liquor

It was the Indian men, however, who made the trading agreements. What they wanted in return for their furs dictated the trade goods the Company stocked at its numerous posts. Knives and guns, axes, flints and steel for fire-making, and traps were by this time considered necessities. Tea was well liked, and so was tobacco, sold usually in twist form. Unfortunately, the big item was liquor. Sometimes it was straight rum, which came from the West Indies via Halifax. But usually the Indians were given a concoction known as "high wine." This was made of pure alcohol, favoured by the Company because it was easy to transport. It was then diluted, sweetened with sugar and fruit extract, and fortified with "oil of vitriol," or sulphuric acid, to give it a convincing kick. The Indians tested any liquor offered them by spitting a mouthful into the fire. If it blazed up, they knew it was strong enough to deserve the name of "firewater". The Indians received from the trade items that they themselves considered of value, but they were far from receiving a significant share of the Company's profits.

The next hierarchy in the Company was that of the voyageurs. Most of them, though not all, were young Canadiens, and for this reason the language of the trade was French, and remained so till the end of the century. They were descendants of voyageurs themselves or attracted to the trade by the voyageur's image of daring, endurance and adventure. A novice would start out as a mere *milieu*, a strong back who sat in the centre of one of the large freight canoes, or *canots du maître*, which made the trip from Montreal, up the Ottawa,

down through Georgian Bay and across Lake Superior. A *milieu* did little but paddle, sixteen hours a day, from daybreak to dusk, with ten-minute stops every hour for a pipe. He would also carry two or three ninety-pound packs across the many steep, muddy, fly-infested portages along the way, supporting them by a tumpline across his forehead. He sang the traditional voyageur songs, which in addition to inspiring nostalgic memories later in the traders or bourgeois seated comfortably amidships, helped him keep time. A good singer got extra pay. He ate three quick meals a day and slept on the ground, wrapped in a blanket, with his head under an overturned canoe if it was raining.

sixty paddle-strokes a minute

If he was good, he might graduate to being an *avant*, the front man who directed the canoe, especially during rapids-shooting, or a *gouvernail*, who stood at the back and steered. He might even become a *guide* or conductor. But his real ambition would be to leave the ranks of the *mangeurs du lard*, so-called because they ate pork instead of pemmican on the spring voyage to Fort William, and become a true *hivernant*, one who spent the winter in the wilderness beyond the fort. These men referred to themselves as *hommes du nord*, and considered themselves tougher, more daring, wiser, and in every way superior to the *mangeurs du lard*. Rivalry between the two was so extreme that fights between them were frequent, and they were made to camp on opposite sides of the Kaministikwia River during the summer gatherings, when the trade goods from Montreal would be exchanged at the fort for the furs gathered during the winter. Even higher in status were the paddlers of express canoes, by which messages were sent and important officials or visitors transported. These men could do sixty paddle-strokes a minute and

A Saulteaux Indian posed for this drawing near the Red River. The tribe, one of many critical to the fur trade, derives its name from its annual gathering at the Sault rapids.

**Cuthbert Grant
Warden of the Plains**

They sang the song in their houses and after the buffalo hunt; a half-century later, Louis Riel, Gabriel Dumont and every proud Métis knew it. The song wove the legend of 23-year-old Cuthbert Grant, their hero and leader, "vanquisher of the haughty British" at the Battle of Frog Plain. That day in 1816, Grant led a party of young Métis against the forces of HBC governor, Robert Semple. When the shooting was over, Semple and 20 of his men were dead, and the war for control of the fur trade between the North West and Hudson's Bay Companies was on. Grant was arrested in 1817 but was released on bail and fled to the West to rejoin the Métis. The shrewd politics of George Simpson, the "little emperor" of the HBC, brought Grant into the Company's fold in 1823, and an annual retainer and the title "Warden of the Plains" kept him in the camp until his death in 1854.

By "hook and crook" and various canoe routes, the wealth of the Northwest found its way into banks of the fur companies.

were the aristocrats among voyageurs.

A voyageur was likely to be worn out by the age of forty, if he had not been drowned in a lake or rapids or killed in a skirmish with a rival company. What did he get in return, besides respect back home? Two suits of clothes a year, in addition to his meagre pay. Food and rum, neither of the best. Support for his Indian or Métis wife and children, even if he should happen to die. Some help on retirement. He supplied his own woven sash, his own beaded pouch for pipe, tobacco and flints and, even more important, his own paddle, lovingly hand-carved and painted red.

It was unlikely, though not completely out of the question, for a voyageur to cross over into the next hierarchy, that of the clerks and traders. Most of these were Highland Scots, though some were

French, some had originally come up from the States, and some, such as Archibald McLeod, were half-breed Indians. Even if you were the nephew of old Simon McTavish, founder of the Company, as William McGillivray was, you were expected to learn the business from the ground up. You would begin as an apprentice-clerk, working in the Montreal warehouses, helping to pack the bundles of trade goods and keep track of the incoming furs. Or you might be posted to Fort William, or even to the true northwest, the country beyond Superior. From apprentice-clerk you could be promoted to clerk (still at very low pay). You might then become a trader, or even a chief trader. Finally, you might become a full partner. If the other partners agreed, you could buy in by purchasing the share of a dead partner or one who wished to resign. Or

Blankets alone were enough to keep these Indians warm as they greet John West, the West's first Anglican missionary.

Robert Semple
Casualty of the Fur War

He didn't really understand just how serious the rivalry was. He was only a businessman. He had travelled the world from Asia Minor to Venezuela, from London to Cape Town. When he became governor of the Hudson's Bay Company in 1815 through the influence of Lord Selkirk, he had little knowledge of the fur trade or British North America. The Red River Settlement was under seige by the Nor'Westers and Métis when Robert Semple arrived, but he still ignored the warnings from friendly Saulteaux Indians and the colony's leader, Colin Robertson. On June 19, he rode out from Fort Douglas with 26 volunteers to parlay with Cuthbert Grant and his band of 60 Métis. He was the new authority and he meant business. But in the interchange someone panicked, a shot was fired, and Semple was dead.

you could be given a share. Partnership entitled you to an equal division of the profits and a voice in the direction of the Company, and it was only at this level that a man could become rich. It was at this level, too, that he could become a member of the Beaver Club and wear his gold medallion.

By the winter of 1817, the members of the Beaver Club had need of their slogan. They were in distress, and they required fortitude. Many of those present at the Mansion House Hotel had just undergone an ignominious journey from Fort William, under arrest and under guard. The trade war with their only remaining rival, the Hudson's Bay Company, which was usually carried on by dosing the Indians with competing amounts of fire-water, had come upsettingly close to resembling a real war, with real battles and real dead bodies. There

had always been the odd backwoods murder, but now the actions of the consumptive and eccentric Lord Selkirk, who had acquired an interest in the Bay through marriage, had escalated matters. The Nor'Westers found this doubly ironic: they had always referred to the Bay, contemptuously, as "the English," but Selkirk, like many of the Hudson's Bay Company factors, was a Highland Scot like themselves. And he had once been an honoured and trusted guest of the Beaver Club. He knew enough about the fur trade to realize that his schemes for settling the Red River Valley with poor Scots, dispossessed by the Highland Clearances, would spell death to the Nor'Westers. He considered himself a high-minded philanthropist, but the Nor'Westers considered him a blackguard and a hypocrite.

The Selkirk settlement's destruction
in 1816 was a result of the intense
fur-trade competition between the
Hudson's Bay Company and the
North West Company.

The Red River area was the principal supply base for the Nor'Westers, the region that produced their all-important pemmican. But settlement would mean houses and fences, a European farmer's way of life. It would mean the depletion of the free-ranging buffalo, the ousting of the Indian and Métis hunters who killed them and an end to the pemmican supplies. To the Métis, it meant white men claiming to *own* land and keeping others off it. With the Red River settled, there would be no fur trade through Montreal, and everyone at the Beaver Club knew it.

the Métis and Indians

The Métis and the Indians knew it too. Their situation was bad, but so was that of the naive settlers themselves, who had been lured to Canada by Selkirk's assurances (despite William McGillivray's advice and anonymous warnings published in the *Inverness Journal*) and deposited at Fort York on Hudson Bay, only to find that almost no preparation had been made for their arrival. They spent the winter of 1812-13 at Fort York, in shelters they had to build themselves. Some starved; others died of scurvy. In the spring they had to trek to the Red River, where again there was no food and no shelter. The Nor'Westers, although they opposed the settlement, felt sorry for the settlers and sent provisions to them.

In 1814 Selkirk's agent, driven to desperation, invoked the Bay monopoly and issued a Pemmican Proclamation confiscating all food in the area – including the North-West Company's supply of pemmican – and forbidding any to be shipped out. There followed a period of skirmishes, arrests and reprisals that ended in 1816 with the Massacre at Seven Oaks in which Selkirk's representative and twenty-one Red River colonists were killed by Métis frontmen for the Nor'Westers. Selkirk held the Nor'Westers responsible and swooped down on Fort William in person with a brigade of Swiss soldiers, seizing the Company partners assembled there for their annual summer gathering. Shipped to Montreal, the partners were easily able to get out on bail. Now, however, they were involved in a quagmire of legal suits and counter-suits that would drag on for years. And they had no reserve capital. They had always divided the profits among themselves and spent it on mansions, food and drink and sumptuous living; for surely the fur trade would go on forever and the money would continue to flow in. Their songs and bottle-smashing at the Mansion House Hotel that winter would have been defiant, but they would have been anxious too. For while they sat in Montreal conferring with their lawyers, Selkirk himself was ensconced in Fort William, rummaging through their papers, sending his men into the surrounding countryside to ransack lesser trading posts and, in his leisure hours, amusing himself by drawing a detailed ground plan of the Fort, which he now considered his. Rumour had it that he'd imprisoned the one remaining partner, old Daniel McKenzie, and had kept him drunk for six weeks until he had signed the entire Fort and its contents over to Selkirk.

the Company's power and riches

What Selkirk had acquired, although illegally, was a miniature, self-sustaining feudal domain. He himself would have occupied one of the four commodious bedrooms opening off the Great Hall. He would have slept in a four-poster bed warmed by a copper warming-pan. He would probably have been waited on by the servants who inhabited the cramped quarters belowstairs, and he may even have eaten food prepared by the Company's own cooks in the adjoining huge kitchen. Every morning, upon arising, he would have strolled through the Great Hall itself, doubtless gloating over his rivals' downfall.

The Great Hall was an impressive structure, but then, it had been built to impress. In it the Company's power and riches were incarnate, as they were in the Beaver Club back in Montreal. It was sixty feet by thirty feet, with a baronial fireplace at each end. It could seat two hundred for dinner. Almost covering one end wall was the gigantic map of the West – the *only* map of the West – drawn by the Company's geographer, David Thompson. All the furnishings needed for a stylish banquet were here, too – silver candlesticks, expensive china, crystal, linen. It was here that the Montreal partners and the wintering partners held their annual feasts, dining on buffalo tongue, lake-trout and whitefish, venison, wild duck and geese, choice wines and spirits, and fresh vegetables from the Fort's own kitchen garden. Just as pemmican was imported for the Beaver Club, here confectionery, packed by the voyageurs all the way from Montreal, was served to finish the meal.

fiddles and bagpipes

Only the top men in the hierarchy sat down to dinner in the Great Hall, but everyone was admitted to the annual ball. Indians, voyageurs, Company clerks and partners all joined in the dances to the music of fiddles and bagpipes. There was also a certain amount of raucous singing and, when everyone was sufficiently warmed up, some Highland flings and sword-dancing. Around midnight there was a gigantic feast, not as luxurious as the dinners but ample nevertheless: cold venison, fish and pork, mountains of bread, hot tea.

Outside the Great Hall were the lesser buildings, also of square-hewn timbers. The Company's aim had been to avoid transportation costs as much as possible, so the Fort contained its own cooperage for making kegs, its own smithy, and its own armoury. It also had its own hospital and a full-time resident doctor, and its own tiny jail,

Lord Selkirk's Diary

Thomas Douglas, a Scottish earl, spent most of his life trying to resettle homeless Highlanders in Canada. His colonies in P.E.I. and Upper Canada failed, and his settlement at the Red and Assiniboine Rivers became the battleground in the struggle between the two fur giants. The Nor'Westers saw the settlement cutting off their line of trade, and their allies, the Métis, saw the colony as a threat to their land claims. Years of gunpowder and trials solved the conflict, but Selkirk never saw the success and died bankrupt.

**Thomas Douglas
Fifth Earl of Selkirk**

The settlement included colonists from Scotland, Switzerland, Germany and French Canada.

Robert Symes, a Hudson's Bay man, is made an honorary chief by a tribe of Indian "partners" in the fur trade. The top hats are appropriate: they were made from beaver pelts, the trade's mainstay.

called the *pot au beurre*, where voyageurs were sent to cool off after a fight. There were canteens for the men and a store for the Indians. There were huge warehouses for furs, trade goods, liquor and ammunition, and, of course, a counting house. There was a kitchen garden and a herb garden for medicines, dyes and preservatives. Outside the fifteen-foot log palisade, with its turrets and lookout tower, were the shipyards and the farm buildings which housed the Fort's sheep, horses, poultry, cows and pigs. The area around the Fort had been cleared of trees and grew hay for the animals and flax for thread and rope. Outside the sturdy main gate were the wharves where the great canoes were loaded.

ideal wives for fur-traders

Selkirk drew all this to scale, meticulously, in black ink, while those left at the Fort watched him fearfully and the Company partners worried in Montreal. In the spring, having done what he could to cripple the Company, he set off for the Red River to make uplifting speeches to the remaining settlers. Then he went off to England, while the legal actions dragged on, draining both his own funds and those of the Company. He died in France in April of 1820, but the damage had been done. The Nor'Westers who had always been at a disadvantage trying to compete with the Bay, were almost bankrupt. They were forced to merge with the Hudson's Bay Company. On the surface it was a coalition of equals. In fact, it was a takeover – the "new" company was the Hudson's Bay Company run from London. Some of the Montreal Nor'Westers got token positions and sinecures. The wintering partners lost their partnerships and became no more than employees, if there were jobs for them at all.

And the women of the fur trade, without whose work there would have been no trade – what was to become of them? It was now many generations since the first French traders had taken Indian wives *à la façon du pays,* in ceremonies that usually involved a bride-price paid to the father and a small party or dance, but no church blessing. The Church did not recognize these marriages, but the Indians and the fur trade did; they were considered strictly honourable, and both the husbands and the North West Company recognized the right of these women and their children to support. High Company officials were not above taking wives in this fashion. William McGillivray himself had a wife called Susan, whose gravestone still stands near Fort William. Sons of these unions were often taken into the fur trade and, like Archibald McLeod, could rise to become partners. Some of the daughters were sent to Quebec to be convent-educated; they usually returned to marry Company men or officials. In fact, the Company had issued a decree in 1806 prohibiting its members from marrying pure-blood Indian women, a decree intended to assure the traders' daughters of a comfortable living. These women were familiar with both worlds, the Indian and the European. Their clothing showed the influence of both, and so did their manners and social accomplishments. Although they never sat at table with their men and, in Indian fashion, served only two meals a day, many would have known how to spin, embroider, and bake bread in a brick bake-oven, as well as the arts of snowshoe-netting and moccasin-making. They were ideal wives for fur-traders.

"bits of Copper"

But the Hudson's Bay Company had always had quite a different attitude towards women of Indian and mixed blood. The officials allowed their men to take Indian wives only grudgingly, and they looked down on both the women and the marriages. After the union of the two companies they introduced missionaries, who looked with horror on these marriages and refused to acknowledge them. And their officials began to marry white women and bring them to the posts, even though they might already have a "summering" wife there. It is not unusual to find Hudson's Bay officials referring in their journals to the women of the fur trade as "bits of Copper." The women on whose labour the vast fortunes of the trade had depended were gradually reduced to inferior status and, if they lived with a trader, came to be regarded as concubines or even prostitutes.

merger

About the only people to gain by the merger were the London-based financiers of the Hudson's Bay Company. Some of the voyageurs were absorbed by the Bay; others, and many clerks and factors, were thrown out of work. Many of the old North West routes and posts were abandoned. The Bay now had an unchallenged monopoly on the fur trade; it no longer had to compete for the furs of the Indians and could set prices as it pleased. Montreal ceased to be the fur-trading capital of North America, and the forty thousand pounds per annum which had once circulated through it as payroll for the North West Company's fifteen hundred employees was gone.

And though some of its individual members went on to build large fortunes elsewhere, the Beaver Club was no more. A half-hearted attempt to revive it was made in 1827, but the spirit which had prompted the midnight songs, the defiant war-whoops and the daring descents from the dining-room table via wine-keg was extinct. Such outbursts had been at least partially due to the hysteria of war, and the war was over. "The lords of the lakes and forests have passed away," said Washington Irving, writing in 1836, "and the hospitable magnates of Montreal – where are they?"

William McGillivray was a partner in the North West Co. and negotiator in the HBC merger. He had five children but only two daughters by his wife Magdeleine, with him above. A man typical of the fur trade, McGillivray fathered offspring by an Indian woman. From such a union came Joseph, Simon and Elizabeth. The boys followed father in the business.

Robert Bouchette contemplates life from inside a Montreal prison, which is palatially furnished for the period. He was even allowed to take his pet bird in with him.

CHAPTER FIVE

Dark and Desperate Crime

This whole frontier district is not only remarkable for the prevalence of vice, but of dark and desperate crime.

Anna Jameson, *Winter Studies and Summer Rambles,* 1838

No one seemed able to agree on how *safe* the colonies were. Was Upper Canada riddled with "ignorance, recklessness, despondency . . . lying and drunkenness," as Anna Jameson had heard; or was it the idyllic spot pictured by Catherine Parr Traill, where no one had to lock his door at night and where no one stole because everyone had enough to eat? Traill took the liberal view that crime was a product of want: eliminate hunger and all will be honest. Jameson's attitude was more conservative: the colonists had been given every advantage, yet despite this, or perhaps because of it, they went to the dogs. But both are united in one thing: what evils there were could be laid in large measure at the door of that demon, Drink.

Becoming an alcoholic, or habitual "drunkard," in the colonies was easy, simply because it was so cheap. In every rural area, a distillery was one of the first businesses to be set up, along with the grist mill and the sawmill. The farmer merely had to cart a few bushels of grain to the distillery and exchange it for whisky by the gallon. In backwoods general stores, whisky was served over the counter, and every town, village and crossroads had its inns and taverns. At barn-raisings and logging bees it was expected that the host would provide whisky by the pailful. The quality of this whisky wasn't high—one traveller refers to it as "Kill the carter"—but it would certainly get you drunk.

There was no tax on whisky in Upper Canada, and the authorities were reluctant to impose one. They were afraid such an act would give rise to illicit stills, and thus to even more "crime and depravity." There were some attempts made, however, to regulate the drinking in taverns and to discourage the local sots. Hours were imposed, and bars—sometimes called "Tippling Houses"—were to be closed on Sundays and on Christmas and Good Friday, except in the case of "travellers." If you were a traveller you could drink whenever you wanted to.

In Halifax and other ports, such as Saint John, New Brunswick, cheap rum from the West Indies took the place of whisky, and the drunks were not settlers on the skids but sailors on a spree or soldiers from the local garrison. In Montreal, it was customary for the voyageurs to go on a binge at Lachine before setting out on their annual trip west. The drunkenness of soldiers, sailors, and voyageurs was in some way traditional and was looked upon with indulgence. In any case, it was sporadic. But the drunkenness of settlers was everywhere condemned, and for a practical reason.

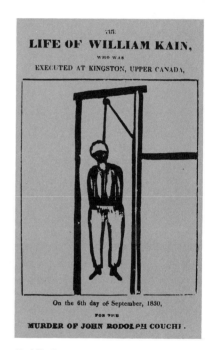

Public hangings were still common when William Kain was executed in 1830. These spectacles attracted large crowds since absence could be interpreted as disloyalty to the Crown. Even women and children convicted of "crime" were dispatched with the "hempen cravatte."

Upper Canada Gazette,

VOL. XV. TORONTO, THURSDAY, DECEMBER 17, 1840. NO. 32

By Authority.

GOVERNMENT HOUSE,
Toronto, 1st October, 1840.

HIS EXCELLENCY the LIEUTENANT-GOVERNOR has been pleased to appoint Mr. John Galt, to be an Inspector of Fish, in the London District.

GOVERNMENT HOUSE,
Toronto, 5th December, 1840.

HIS EXCELLENCY THE LIEUTENANT-GOVERNOR has been pleased to appoint Henry Solomon Reid, Esquire, to be Collector of Duties and Customs, at and for the Ports of Bond Head Harbour, and Port Darlington, in this Province.

GOVERNMENT HOUSE,
12th December, 1840.

HIS EXCELLENCY THE LIEUTENANT-GOVERNOR has been pleased to accept the resignation of Mr. Ezra William Holton, as an Inspector of Beef and Pork, in the District of Victoria.

P R O C L A M A T I O N.
UPPER CANADA.
GEO. ARTHUR.

VICTORIA, *by the Grace of GOD, of the United Kingdom of Great Britain and Ireland, QUEEN, Defender of the Faith, &c. &c. &c.*

To all to whom these presents shall come—

GREETING:

WHEREAS it hath been humbly represented to Us, that on Monday, the 26th day of October, now last past, a most brutal and atrocious Assault and *Rape* was committed upon the person of *Elizabeth Johnson,* the Wife of Alanson Johnson, of the Township of Wilmot, in the District of Wellington, of our Province of Upper Canada, Labourer, by an *Indian* of the name of KA-KAS-SEP, otherwise called JACOB COOK-A-DIN-NA.

Now KNOW YE, That for the better apprehending and bringing to Justice the perpetrator of so heinous an offence, a Reward of T W E N T Y - F I V E P O U N D S, of lawful money of our said Province, will be paid to any person or persons, who shall cause the said Ka-Kas-Sep, otherwise called Jacob Cook-a-din-na, to be taken into custody, and

brought before one of our Justices of the Peace, to answer for the said Crime.

IN TESTIMONY WHEREOF, We have caused these our Letters to be made Patent, and the Great Seal of our said Province to be hereunto affixed: WITNESS, our trusty and well-beloved SIR GEORGE ARTHUR, K. C. H. Lieutenant-Governor of our said Province, and Major-General Commanding our Forces therein, at Toronto, this twelfth day of December, in the year of our Lord one thousand eight hundred and forty, and in the fourth year of our Reign.

G. A.

By Command of His Excellency in Council.
R. A. TUCKER,
32-n SECRETARY.

P R O C L A M A T I O N.
UPPER CANADA.
GEO. ARTHUR.

VICTORIA, *by the Grace of GOD, of the United Kingdom of Great Britain and Ireland, Queen, Defender of the Faith, &c. &c. &c.*

To all to whom these presents shall come—

GREETING:

WHEREAS by an Act of the Parliament of the Province of Upper Canada, passed in the eighth year of the reign of His late Majesty King George the Fourth, entitled, " An Act to confer upon His Majesty certain powers and authorities necessary to the making, maintaining and using the Canal, intended to be completed under His Majesty's direction, for connecting the waters of Lake Ontario with the River Ottawa, and for other purposes therein-mentioned," it is amongst other things enacted, "That all persons whatsoever shall have free liberty to navigate the said Canal with any Boats, Barges, Vessels or Rafts, upon payment of such rates and dues as shall be established by His Majesty": *And whereas* by our Royal Proclamation, under the Great Seal of our said Province, bearing date at Toronto, the twelfth day of May, in the year of our Lord one thousand eight hundred and thirty-six, and in the sixth year of the reign of our late Royal Predecessor, We did establish and authorise to be imposed

on all persons navigating the said Canal, with any Boats, Barges, Vessels or Rafts, certain rates and dues therein-mentioned, to be exacted, levied and collected, and for our use, during our pleasure: *And whereas* We have thought fit to alter the rates and dues thereby established, and to authorise the rates and dues hereinafter mentioned to be levied in their stead.—Now KNOW YE, That of our certain knowledge, mere motion and special grace, We have established, and do hereby establish and authorise to be imposed upon all persons navigating the said Canal with any Boats, Barges, Vessels or Rafts, in lieu of the rates and dues heretofore authorised to be taken as aforesaid, the rates and dues following, that is to say : from By-town to Kingston, and from Kingston to Bytown—

Cabin Passengers, 4s. each.
Children under 12 years of age, 2s. each.
Neat Cattle and Horses, 4s. each.
Sheep, Pigs, and Calves, 6d. each.
Dry Goods, Wines and Spirituous Liquors, 7s. 6d. per ton.
Iron and Salted Fish, 3s. 9d. per ton.
Salt and Sea Coal, 1s. 10d. per ton.
Wheat per bushel, three farthings.
Other kinds of Grain and Potatoes, per bushel, one farthing.
Rye and Buck-wheat Flour, and Corn Meal, per bushel, one half-penny.
Hay, passing one or more Locks, 2s. 6d. per ton.
Flour, per barrel, 2½d.
Beef and Pork, per barrel, 3½d.
Pot Ash, per ton, 2s. 3d.
Pearl Ash, per ton, 2s. 3d.
Oak, per foot, in boats or scows, one half-penny.
Pine, Elm, and all soft timber, per foot, in boats or scows, one farthing.
The same in rafts, namely—
    Oak, one penny per cubic foot.
    Pine, one farthing per cubic foot.
Standard Staves, 20s. per 1000.
The same in boats or scows, 10s. per 1000.
West India Staves, 3s. 4d. per 1000.
The same in boats or scows, 1s. 8d. per 1000.
Heading, per 1000, 1s. 3d.
Deals, per 1000 feet, in rafts, 2s. 6d.
The same in boats and scows, 1s. 6d.
Boards and Planks, per 1000 feet, in rafts, 2s. 6d.
The same in boats or scows, 1s. 6d.
Shingles, per 1000, 3d.
Laths, sawed or split, per 1000, 3d.
Saw Logs passing from one to three Locks, 1d. each Log.
Saw Logs passing from four to six Locks, 2d. each Log.

Cast among the endless notices of the sales of crown and clergy lands, the official government journal, Upper Canada Gazette, *made notice of crimes. The rapist, if caught, was probably hung.*

A man struggling to clear his farm and pay off his debts simply could not afford the time off to get drunk. About the only good thing that could be said about the use of alcohol by the poor was that it appeared to be healthier than water, especially in time of epidemics. Since no one knew about germs or pollution, no one boiled the water, which might come from a sewage-tainted well, a stream that flowed through a graveyard, or a lake where garbage was dumped. It was observed that those who drank nothing but beer lived longer. Liquor might ruin you, but it wouldn't kill you outright.

"Drunk as a lord"

On the other hand, if you were from the right social class, it was *déclassé* not to drink. "Drunk as a lord" still had meaning, and the image of the hard-drinking Regency buck lingered on well past the Regency. A "gentleman" could almost have been defined as someone who could afford to get drunk regularly, and many did. To be a teetotaller was to be irrevocably middle-class, and, to the Tories of Upper Canada, even moderation smacked of Methodism, unhealthy radical views and general scoundreliness. A man who did not drink was not to be trusted. Ladies, of course, did not drink to excess. They rose after dinner and gathered in the drawing-room, sipping tea, while the gentlemen lit their pipes and passed the port and brandy.

Being drunk was viewed as a vice rather than a crime. But the list of things that were crimes was long, and so was the list of punishments. You could be thrown into jail for being a deserter from the army or navy, even though you might have been pressed into service against your will. You could be jailed for being a runaway apprentice, even though your master, who virtually owned you during your term of apprenticeship, had beaten and starved you. Furthermore, you could be prosecuted for helping or harbouring either a deserter or a runaway apprentice, servant, or slave – slavery was not formally abolished by the British Parliament till 1833 – and the newspapers of the time are peppered with such notices. The threat of prosecution, and sometimes the promise of a reward, must have made escape difficult for runaways.

You could be jailed for a debt, even a trifling one of five shillings, though in this case your creditor had to supply a daily pittance for your food; if he forgot to send the money, you were automatically free. If you were declared an habitual pauper, however, your fate might be worse. England had the Poorhouses, and the Poor-Laws to support them, but the Poorhouses cost taxpayers money. Nova Scotia wished to avoid what it viewed as an unnecessary expense, so until 1837 it held Paupers' Auctions. The paupers were auctioned off to bidders who wanted cheap labour. Whoever claimed to be able to support the pauper for the smallest sum would win the pauper, who was forbidden to run away. The government paid the maintenance price, and the pauper would be worked to death on a starvation diet.

orphans for sale

Orphans were sometimes auctioned off in this way as well since no one seemed to know what else to do with them. In rural areas, if your parents had died or been killed in an accident, it was likely that some neighbouring family would take you in. But children of the poor in cities or children of immigrants who had died aboard ship would be stranded. If they were in Montreal and very lucky, the nuns might take them in. Otherwise they might become beggars, or they might starve to death. Or, if they came to the attention of the government, they might be put in jail, where they would at least get some bread and water. There were no orphanages in Upper Canada until 1834. Insane asylums were scarce, too, so the insane and even the retarded

were also usually jailed, and their families had to pay for their maintenance.

professional thieves

The most frequently punished crime in the colonies was stealing. Sailors in Halifax stole housewives' washing off the line, starving children stole loaves of bread, servants stole bits of velvet ribbon. In Montreal, in 1815, someone stole a number of "Brass Knockers" from the fronts of houses; no one knew why. Horses and gold and silver watches were frequent targets. So were silver snuff boxes. In November, just in time for winter, someone made off with a "Dark Bottle Green GREAT COAT" from Montreal's City Tavern.

But professional thieves aimed for larger prizes. Before banks were generally established – there was no bank in Montreal before 1817, and the twenties saw the establishment of banks in Upper Canada and the Maritimes – merchants kept their money on their business premises, locked in heavy iron strongboxes. Sometimes the thieves were unable to pry the boxes open, but more often they succeeded. Another favourite commodity was tobacco, as in the sad case of John G. Beek, Esquire, whose cellar was "burgularously broken into" by a set of "audacious villains," who not only escaped with the "Manufactured Tobacco" but almost set the house on fire. Locks, chains, bolts and bars festooned merchants' houses and offices, for in those days, when men often gambled their capital on one shipment of one commodity, a small trader could be ruined by a single theft. The *Montreal Herald*, commenting on one such crime, indicated "the necessity of establishing a more rigid system of police for the better protection of the lives and property of the citizens."

Systems of police were indeed not very rigid. Some cities had no regular police force at all; they might have a night watch, or a patrol, but almost

ATTENTION!!! THE Subscriber is under the necessity of calling on all those indebted to him by note or otherwise, whose accounts have been standing over eight months, for a settlement of the same.
N. B. If the above notice is not attended to soon, I will positively make cost.
STEWART WILSON.
S. W. Still keeps on hand a constant supply of Wagons, Ploughs &c. &c. which he will dispose of on a years credit.
Hallowell, Oct. 18. 1831.

Merchants like Stewart Wilson faced no small problem when they made an attempt to collect accounts that were overdue. Their only recourse was to take the debtor to court – an expensive process, and one that could offend other customers. Mr. Wilson tried to play it safe by including an advertisement for a year's credit to new customers in this attention grabbing notice.

no investigative police work was done. Some owners, instead of relying on the law, offered rewards for the return of their property "with no questions asked." A clever professional thief could do quite well for himself.

bread and water

As usual, it was the amateurs who frequently got caught. Once in the hands of the law, you were in for no easy time. If you were arrested on suspicion and could not raise bail, you might be held for trial six months or a year. If you had no money of your own, you might be given the option of starving to death, or of grinding flour on the treadmill in order to pay for your own food. The food would be the same as that eaten by convicted prisoners. It was, literally, bread and water, though if you had some money you'd be free to spend it on extras. Luckily for the prisoners, the bread was brown bread, and you were allowed a pound and a half of it a day; but the quality wasn't likely to be high, as the contract for supplying the jail-bread was bid for and the lowest tender got it. The jailer, too, was likely to skimp on the supplies. He was allowed a set amount of money for running the entire operation, out of which he had to pay himself and his turnkeys. Obviously, he'd be tempted to augment his own salary at the prisoners' expense.

In the jail itself, which was probably overcrowded and dilapidated, you were likely to find yourself in a dark, damp cell so small you could hardly lie down in it, with little heat in winter, no bed – if you were lucky, you might get some straw, but even that would probably be old, dirty and louse-infested – no means of washing yourself, and not much ventilation. The stench would be overpowering. In 1838, a Grand Jury in Upper Canada recommended a daily "fumigation" with vinegar and asked also that "insane persons" should be removed "as nauseous effluvia proceeded from the

apartments of these unfortunate beings." The Grand Jury – whose duty it was to inspect the jail, but which had no power to change anything – also recommended a yearly whitewashing of the cells to keep down the lice, "and make the walls a less moving scene." Typhus fever, transmitted from infected prisoners by lice – although nobody knew this – was so common in jails that it was known as "gaol fever." Women and children as young as eight were stuck in with everyone else; there were no separate women's quarters in Upper Canada until the 1830s. You might be shackled, chained or manacled. You might get a single blanket to wrap yourself in, or you might not. You would wear your own clothes till they fell apart, after that, there was usually no provision made for giving you any more. No wonder there were occasional prison "riots and routs," though those taking part in them were often punished by whipping, torture and solitary confinement.

punishments

All this could happen to you even before your trial. At the trial itself, your guilt might be determined by a jury, but your fate would be decided by the magistrates who passed sentence. Magistrates were appointed by the Crown and were, of course, drawn from the upper classes. Few questioned the right of the moneyed classes to protect their "lives and property" from those without money, just as few questioned the prevalent feeling that people committed crimes because they were innately evil. Punishments were as public as possible, to serve as a warning to others and as example to small children and to identify the criminal so he could be shunned by all right-thinking people.

Sentencing was brutal. For petty theft, you could undergo branding or "burning in the hand." For this, you were marched into the courtroom and your hand was fastened to the dock, palm

The right to collect tolls on a toll road often went to the highest bidder. Toll gates every few miles were a nuisance and grievance in both Upper and Lower Canada, the toll collector generally lining his own pockets well before paying the government's share.

Candidates and voters square off at a Perth, U.C. polling booth. Elections were often drunken, violent affairs since votes were cast by standing and declaring a candidate's name. If the opponent's men were drunk or numerous enough, the voter might receive a sound thrashing for standing for the wrong man.

open. You were told that as soon as the hot iron – sometimes a crown, sometimes a letter, such as *T* for *thief* – touched you, you should repeat "Vive le roi" three times, or "God Save the King" if you were English. As one commentator ironically remarked, this was sure to make you extremely loyal. As soon as you'd done this, the iron would be removed, but you would have the mark for the rest of your life.

hanged for stealing a cow

In addition, you could be sentenced to be whipped, lashed or flogged. You would be taken to a public place, such as the market, or have your hands tied to a cart. Men and women alike were stripped to the waist, a fact that outraged later moralists. Whipping, like branding, was done by the hangman, who was also on hand if you were to be pilloried. In this case your head and hands were stuck through holes in a wooden platform which could be turned to make you face the people in the marketplace. The sadists and the self-righteous in the crowd could amuse themselves by throwing rotten eggs, mud, vegetables and rocks at you, while the hangman whipped you from behind to keep you facing the front.

For more serious offences you might be banished (one woman was banished in York in 1834, for "keeping a disorderly house"), transported to Australia or the "Bermudas," or hanged. But as there were over a hundred capital offences, the magistrates could usually find grounds for hanging you if they felt like it, and they often did. In Montreal, in 1813, a thirteen-year-old boy was hanged for stealing a cow. In 1815, a man was hanged for shoplifting. But in 1822, two men convicted of murder were merely "burned on the hand," whereas in the following year a man was hanged for stealing "three horses, a cow and heifer." The last execution for cattle-stealing took place in 1829, and in the same year two men were hanged for "sacrilege."

Once you'd been condemned, the government hanged you at once. They didn't want you wasting your time and theirs in a vain search for a reprieve, so they usually set the date two or three days from the day of sentencing. Hangings were public, and they were attended not only by the rabble, eager for sensation, but also by the quality, probably also eager for sensation but disguising their interest as morality. To attend a hanging was to show approval of the sentence and to reinforce the law. In the early years of the century, hangings were usually packed. You were hanged from a scaffold or gibbet, where everyone could get a good look at you. The hangman, who did not adopt the custom of wearing a black hood until the 1830s, was a permanent fixture of the court, usually a condemned criminal who had bought his life by taking on the job. Once you had been pronounced dead, the hangman was entitled to your clothes and to the rope, both of which he could cut up and sell for souvenirs. Your body belonged to the State.

hard-drinking society

It was common practice for the bodies of criminals to be handed over to a medical doctor for dissection; in fact, they provided almost the only legal supply of corpses during the period. After the dissection, the doctor and his medical students were supposed to cut the body up into small pieces for disposal. A bizarre variation of this procedure took place near Perth in 1829. A settler named Thomas Easby murdered his wife and four children, then set fire to his house to conceal the evidence. He was discovered, tried, convicted and hanged. Before the customary dissection, the body, for some reason which history does not record, was skinned. The skin was then tanned and cut into convenient squares, which were peddled

William Johnston
Pirate of the St. Lawrence

From one of a thousand secret havens in Upper Canada's Thousand Islands, William Johnston and his crew of pirates plundered passing ships and ransacked coastal villages. It was all in the name of revenge. Born in Trois Rivières, L.C., in 1782, he was jailed by the British in 1812 for aiding Americans. After he escaped across Lake Ontario, his property was confiscated and his family was left impoverished without his support. Bitter, cruel and ruthless, he became a spy for the Yankees and quickly became notorious as a pirate and smuggler. In 1838, after the collapse of the rebellions in the Canadas, Johnston enlisted to command the Patriot "navy." His greatest coup came when he and his band captured the British paddle wheeler, *Sir Robert Peel*, ran it aground, burned it and escaped with $100,000 booty.

to the public at $2.00 each.

But already things were changing. The law, harsh as it was, was responsive to public opinion. In the 1830s, public sentiment towards crime underwent a widespread change. The old attitudes were dying out. The hard-drinking, punitive Tory society, with its assumptions about the original sinfulness of criminals, especially poor criminals, was on the wane. The old way had been to refuse to help those on the way down, and to kick them very hard once they had reached the bottom. Now, people were slowly beginning to realize that crime and vice flourished in a poverty-stricken environment, and that the richer classes might be, at least to some extent, their brothers' keepers.

The first Tory custom to weaken was drinking. Temperance Societies and Methodism were on the increase, and though the reformers were not able to abolish taverns, they did change the image of "gentleman." It became unfashionable in polite society to be drunk as a lord. Some urged total abstinence, though a wistful voice was heard here and there, urging moderation instead. Major Strickland, Catherine Parr Traill's brother, based his argument on the Bible: "Throughout the whole Bible and Testament, there is not a single command to abstain totally from either wine or strong drink. Then in respect to the prohibition, the false prophet has, in the Koran, forbidden his followers to use wine at all. Now, which do we profess to follow – the precepts of Jesus Christ, or those of Mahomet?"

There was a decrease in public punishments and public hangings. The pillory and the stocks gradually faded away, and death sentences were often commuted to imprisonments, flogging or transportation. Magistrates who had once dispensed hangings with a free hand became more wary, for popular sentiment had changed. In Montreal in 1829, when three men were hanged for ox-stealing, the mob almost hanged the hangman himself for bungling the job. In Upper Canada, at Long Point, in 1831, the hangman used too thin a rope and only half-hanged the condemned man. The rope broke, and the victim staggered around in circles until he was strung up again. Once more, public feeling was outraged. And in 1883, in Nova Scotia, the crowd was so aroused by a botched job that it attempted to run the hangman out of town on a rail. It wasn't that people were against the death sentence; but they were turning against the spectacle, which was now considered uncivilized. Consequently, the number of offences for which you could be hanged was reduced in 1833 from over a hundred to twelve.

There was a clamour, too, for improvements in jail conditions. Women must have their own jails, to keep them from depravity. Men must be given soup as well as bread. A prisoner without clothes was an outrage to modesty. The most advanced thinkers felt that criminals should no longer be shut up and tortured: they should be put to some useful work, to improve their characters. And a scientific outlook was becoming fashionable. Crime was no longer to be viewed as the result of Original Sin alone. The phrenological opinion was that it was the result of an overdeveloped bump of criminality on one's skull. Ladies had once visited prisons as an amusement, and this was still possible. You could visit the Kingston Penitentiary, built in 1835, for a small fee, "male adults 1 shilling and threepence each, females and children seven and a half pence." Increasingly, however, the visitors arrived armed with tracts and Bibles, to exhort the prisoners to a better life. Even before the advent of Victoria, Victorian morality, with its emphasis on duty, chastity, sobriety and usefulness, was on its way in.

William Bowie
Victim of a Duel

On the morning of July 21, 1819, two young men stood back-to-back at Fort Needham near Halifax, Nova Scotia. When the signal was given, they took their paces, turned and fired their pistols, and one man dropped. The issue was one of slander, said the newspapers, and although duelling had been outlawed for some time and was punishable by hanging, Mr. Justice William Haliburton found Richard Uniacke *not guilty*. In his reading of the law, the death penalty had never been inflicted "where the conduct of the parties had been fair and honourable." William Bowie was a Halifax merchant; Richard Uniacke was the son of the attorney general.

Hunters and Traders

The Nootkas of Vancouver Island were expert whalers; the coastal tribes were skilled fishermen and hunters of elk, moose and bear, and traded among themselves. The Plains tribes—Cree, Blackfoot and Assiniboin— hunted buffalo and trapped pelt animals for trade with fur company factors. The Ojibwa dominated the trade north of the Lakes, and the Micmacs and Malecites still traded only when they needed white man's goods.

Captain Andrew Bulger, governor of Assiniboia, meets Chippewa warriors and chiefs at Fort Douglas, on the site of Winnipeg. The fort was a Hudson's Bay trading post, and the Indians were both customers and suppliers. After the merger with the Nor'Westers in 1821, the HBC replaced Fort Douglas with Fort Garry.

This Micmac band has chosen what it wants from the white man's world—guns, traps and axes—and retained Indian tools for a hunting and fishing: canoes and portable shelter. Crosses around the women's necks show that missionaries have visited along with traders: in return, whites learned to use toboggans and snowshoes.

FALLS OF NIAGARA.

Above, below, where'er the astonished eye
Turns to behold, new opening wonders lie,

With uproar hideous, first the *Falls* appear,
The stunning tumult thundering on the ear.

There the broad river, like a lake outspread,
The islands, rapids, falls, in grandeur dread.

This great, o'erwhelming work of awful Time,
In all its dread magnificence, sublime.

A Feeling Bosom

Who has not had a wish t'inspect Niagara's famed cataract? The scenery around inspires, and every feeling bosom fires.

J. L. Alexander, "Wonders of the West, & etc, a poem," 1825

Was there anyone in polite society who had not had a wish to inspect Niagara Falls? If so, he would not have dared to admit it. This was no longer the eighteenth century, whose representative man, Dr. Samuel Johnson, would not have given two pins for a lot of water going over a cliff. Burke had first defined the picturesque, but some of the most idolized poets of the day had spread the gospel. Readers of taste praised Byron's *Childe Harold's Pilgrimage.* Like young Joe Howe of Nova Scotia, educating himself after his long hours at the printing press, they also admired Sir Walter Scott, and those extremely popular lyricists, Campbell, Moore, and Mrs. Felicia Hemans. Scenery, especially rugged, grandiose, *sublime* scenery, was the thing, and one's taste in gnarled trees was, in the finer circles, almost as important in establishing one's place in the social order as one's taste in gloves, horses or bonnets. Jane Austen satirized this fashion through Edward Ferrars, a young man with more sense than sensibility

Remember I have no knowledge in the picturesque, and I shall offend you by my ignorance and want of taste if we come to particulars. I shall call hills steep which ought to be bold; surfaces strange and uncouth which ought to be irregular and rugged; and distant objects out of sight which ought to be indistinct through the soft medium of a hazy atmosphere

But the fashion flourished despite Jane. The great thing was to have a feeling bosom, and to be known to have one; one, moreover, that could be fired by the approved objects. Not to have a feeling bosom might open one to the charge of being a mere shopkeeper at heart.

Niagara Falls was the number-one bosom-firer of the early nineteenth century. No pleasure-trip in eastern North America was complete without a visit to the Falls, and by the twenties, a tourist industry was already established. Lower Canadians and Maritimers approached up the St. Lawrence from Montreal, and by 1825 they could take steamboats almost all the way, with short journeys by stage-coach around the unnavigable rapids. Americans came up the Erie Canal or from Albany by coach. Already there were guide books, such as Theodore Dwight's *The Northern Traveller,* "of a convenient pocket size, embellished with nineteen maps and eight illustrations," in which the tourist unsure of his own taste could look up which pieces of landscape to admire, and, on a more practical level, which routes to take and which hotels to stay in. On the "British" side of the Falls, preferred by connoisseurs, there were two

Third class metal tokens were the fare in 1837, when the Montreal and Lachine Railroad Company launched its service over seven-and-a-half miles of track. The line was built to bypass the Lachine rapids.

Opposite page: Niagara Falls, *by Edward Hicks, is typical of the many artistic tributes to the famous cataract. Poets praised it, and visitors to Upper Canada went far to see it.*

**Oliver Goldsmith
The Other Oliver Goldsmith**

Oliver Goldsmith of St. Andrews,
New Brunswick was the great-nephew
of Oliver Goldsmith, the Irish poet
and author of *The Deserted Village.*
After trying his hand at various odd
jobs, he entered his father's career
as a soldier. He had some interest
in books, and in Halifax he became
friends with Joseph Howe. Like many
other career soldiers he also took
some part in garrison theatricals
and in 1822 played the role of Tony
Lumpkin in his great-uncle's play,
She Stoops To Conquer. His first
and only book, the long lyrical
poem, *The Rising Village,* brought
him little popularity and is in fact
an attempt at adapting his uncle's
poetic style to his own writing.
Goldsmith never wrote more than a
few poems, and spent the rest of his
life posted in exotic British ports
like Hong Kong and Corfu.

Montmorency Falls, near Quebec City, drew troupes of picnicking sightseers in the summer, and sleigh riders in winter.

large hotels. Forsyth's was the recommended one,
because of the "fine view of the cataract" from the
galleries and windows in the rear. Visitors were
urged to visit the Falls as often as possible, standing on Table Rock for "*the finest* view," and de-
scending a spiral staircase supported by a ship's
mast for "the most sublime view," from below.
There, drenched by spray, all but "persons with
weak lungs" could explore the cavern beneath the
Falls and contemplate the "terrible abyss" beyond. Surely no one could return from such an excursion with bosom unfired.

Some did, though; but you had to be very sure
of your own social status to confess it. "Tyger"
Dunlop sat on the edge of Table Rock with his
legs dangling over, blessing his stars that he "was
not one to be thrown into ecstacies and raptures
merely because other people had been so." However, when he saw two men fishing below and real-

ized how high the Falls really were, he did a quick
back somersault away from the edge. No such moment of truth ever struck the peripatetic gentlewoman Anna Jameson, for whom the Falls was
one of the biggest disappointments of her life. Part
of the difficulty may have been that she made her
trip in winter; part may have been due to the enormous expectations which had been aroused by the
rhapsodies of others. "The reality," she lamented,
"has displaced from my mind an illusion far more
magnificent than itself." But some of her disappointment might have been prompted by the deli-
cately snobbish pleasure of refusing to be impressed by a sight so universally praised. "I have
beheld them, and shall I whisper it to you? – but, O
tell it not among the Philistines – I wish I had not!"

Sublime scenery was not the only thing valued,
undervalued and again re-valued by the sensitive
tourist. In fact, the early-nineteenth-century ideas

It may never have looked this romantic, but the Rideau Canal was impressive, dropping through eight locks to the Ottawa.

**John By
The Colonel of Bytown**

of what constituted tourist attractions were not that different from our own: stunning scenery, historical sites, local colour. Battlefields, especially battlefields where eminent persons had died, were held to be of interest, and Dwight directs attention to Queenston Heights and the death of Brock, and of course to the Plains of Abraham and the deaths of Wolfe and Montcalm. Archeology and anthropology were in their infancy, but Indian burial grounds were already felt to be worthy of inspection. Near the residence of Sir Peregrine Maitland, for instance, there were some "Ancient Tumuli," where the blowing down of a tree had revealed "a great number of skeletons. . . with Indian beads, pipes, &c. and some conch-shells shaped apparently for musical instruments." People could be picturesque too: in Europe, Highland Scots, Italian banditti, and gypsies were much in favour. But Canada had even more to offer. The voyageurs

were certainly picturesque, and so, to some extent, were Canadien peasants, who had the added attraction of being considered exceptionally polite. (Recently imported Irish peasants were not picturesque. Neither, away from the Scotland of Sir Walter, were Scots.) But the Indians were more picturesque than any imaginable competition, and many a paragraph was devoted to their romantic virtues, followed inevitably by another paragraph lamenting their passing.

Displaying one's knowledge of the picturesque, however, was not the only motive for writing about the scenery. Not everyone could travel. Most people passed their lives without ever leaving their own country, some without leaving their own city or town. Consequently there was an enormous hunger for vicarious experience, and if you took the trouble to write a letter or keep a journal, you could be sure that your friends or family would

Instead of a knighthood, a pension and a comfortable retirement, John By was called up on the royal carpet to face charges of extravagance in building the Rideau Canal. He was a sensitive, chubby, red-faced man, a military engineer who had worked in Quebec for ten years. In 1826, he took on the task of building a 126-mile canal from Kingston to the fork of the Ottawa and Rideau Rivers. Rather than the usual "ditch and tow" method of most canals, he devised a system of hydraulic locks, dams and channels. The project was completed in 1832, but not before he had so angered the Colonial Office with his expenses that they threatened to kill the dream. When the village on the Rideau grew up to be a town, it was called Bytown; and when the town later became Ottawa, John By's prediction that "the hill would one day house public buildings" came true.

read it appreciatively, not once but many times. There was a large public audience, too, for this kind of writing, and both British and Canadian readers devoured travel books almost as enthusiastically as they devoured Scott's novels. Travel itself was romantic: Lord Byron did it. It was an adventure, and adventures were already prized in a society that was beginning to feel deprived of them. It was no longer so obvious as it had been to Dr. Johnson that cities and civilization were unmixed blessings.

stretches of corduroy

But although travel was romantic, the process of actually doing it in the Canadas was not. It was almost mandatory to describe the horrors of the trip—the hideous Canadian roads, the wretched Canadian inns—as it was to describe delights of the landscape. Considering the pain of all kinds inflicted on the travellers, it's amazing that anyone went anywhere at all.

Sight-seeing for its own sake was of course the prerogative of the rich. If you had little money, you travelled only if you had to. You could not afford a stagecoach or a steamboat, so you rode on horseback. If you were even poorer, you walked. But money would not necessarily protect you from unpleasant sensations. A stagecoach fare would buy you a jolting ride over roads dusty and rutted when dry, boggy when wet, with stretches of corduroy—logs laid side by side—which dislocated every bone in your body. The coaches had no springs and were suspended from the axles by long strips of rivetted leather, so the coach would sway and lurch nauseatingly whenever the horses were allowed to go faster than a trot. In spring and early summer, clouds of mosquitoes assailed the traveller, especially when the coach stopped every fifteen miles to change the exhausted horses. Bridges over streams and rivers were made of wood and had the nasty habit of rotting out, collapsing sometimes just when the coach was going across. And coaches were slow: even over a "good" road, the average speed was seven-and-a-half miles an hour, allowing for stops. It was better to go by sleigh in winter, but then you might freeze in the inns.

Water travel, in almost anything that could float, was much preferred to the hellish Canadian roads. Young Lieutenant Coke spent his 1832 furlough floating down the St. Lawrence en route from Quebec to New Brunswick, "to kill time." He couldn't take the steamer because of the cholera quarantine, so he rented an open pilot-boat and laid in a supply of those things deemed necessary for the traveller: a bottle of laudanum, a box of opium pills, a bottle of eau-de-Cologne and another of eau-de-vie. He spent the first evening playing upon his flute, but on the second night it rained, and the fog was so thick the pilot refused to go ashore. Undaunted, Coke rummaged through his portmanteau and pulled on "two pair of trowsers, a seal-skin cap and hat, two coats, and a seal-skin jacket, with hood like that of an Esquimaux." All of these layers of fur and cloth became drenched. "I was so encumbered with the weight of my heavy apparel that, had the boat swamped, I should have gone to the bottom like a lump of lead. . . . The only active service I could perform was to sit at the bottom of the boat, wrenching the rain out of my cap and jacket, or take a turn at bailing out the water."

notebooks and sketchbooks

Anna Jameson fared somewhat better on her tour of Lake Huron. She too went in a hired boat, but it was a canoe, propelled by sturdy and "picturesque" voyageurs, who always put her tent up first when it rained. She reclined on the bottom of the canoe, with a pillow at her back, and was

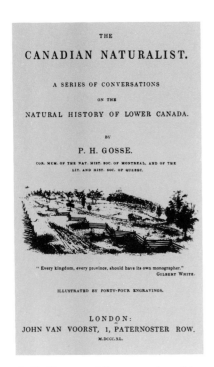

THE
CANADIAN NATURALIST.

A SERIES OF CONVERSATIONS

ON THE

NATURAL HISTORY OF LOWER CANADA.

BY

P. H. GOSSE.

COR. MEM. OF THE NAT. HIST. SOC. OF MONTREAL, AND OF THE
LIT. AND HIST. SOC. OF QUEBEC.

" Every kingdom, every province, should have its own monographer."
GILBERT WHITE.

ILLUSTRATED BY FORTY-FOUR ENGRAVINGS.

LONDON:
JOHN VAN VOORST, 1, PATERNOSTER ROW.
M.DCCC.XL.

P. H. Gosse took "sweet and soothing pleasures" from rambles in the Canadian wilds, and recorded his personal observations on its flora and fauna.

quite comfortable, especially since she had by her side "my cloak, umbrella, and parasol, my note-books and sketch-books, and a little compact basket. . . containing eau-de-Cologne, and all those necessary luxuries that may be wanted in a moment." The parasol and the Cologne may be faintly ludicrous, but Mrs. Jameson was considered brave. White women were not supposed to go that far off the beaten track. When Anna insisted on shooting rapids in a canoe, for the delightful "sensation," another thing unheard-of for a white woman, the Indians were delighted with her.

upriver to Montreal

It was more orthodox to travel by steamboat. By 1815, the Molsons, who had already done very well with their brewery, were running three steam boats between Montreal and Quebec, the *Accommodation*, the *Swiftsure* and the *Malsham*. The trip cost twelve dollars in the cabin, about a third of that in the steerage, and, if you wanted to take your dog, a dollar extra. The trip upriver to Montreal took slightly over twenty-four hours, and four meals were provided. The steamboats had not attained the elaboration of style and design that was later to earn them the name of "floating hotels," but they were certainly more agreeable than the stagecoaches. Molson's regulations indicate that the travellers were of all classes, and that rowdy behaviour was frequent enough to require some control:

The after Cabin is exclusively for the Ladies, their children and female servants. . . smoking in the Cabin and spitting on the floor are prohibited; but persons may smoke on deck. No person is to go to bed with boots or shoes on — All gaming is to cease at 10 at night, and no kind of liquors will be served after that hour, that those persons who wish to sleep may not be disturbed. — Sitting on the tables is prohibited. Every

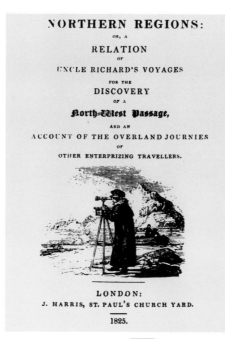

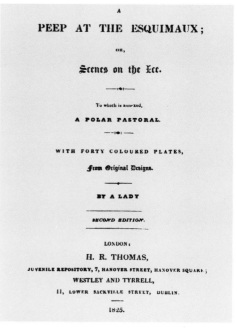

Esquimaux

The only white men to set eyes on the Eskimo in this period were Arctic explorers like John Franklin, Edward Parry and James Clark Ross. Europeans knew only one kind of Eskimo, the travel writer's kind that lived in igloos, paddled in kayaks, and hunted strange creatures of the sea. It was a world of ice with very little culture, a solid wall that stood in the way of a direct passage to the Orient. The few travellers who visited the Arctic printed these "peeps."

Couriers on the 636-mile Halifax to Quebec City run had to make "post haste," and had to explain delays. In the days of corduroy roads and miles of mud, it must have been a thankless task.

kind of injury done by passengers to the paintings, furniture, breakage of Chrystal and China Ware &c. [sic] must be paid for.

Steamboats had another advantage: you didn't have to stay at an inn. Although there were several exclusive hotels in Montreal, one at York, and a couple at Niagara Falls, good inns were rare along the stagecoach routes. In Nova Scotia the inns were rated by travellers according to the kind of sugar they served. The best, which were likely also to have the most comfortable beds and the cleanest bedrooms, served white sugar. Second-rate inns were known as "brown-sugar houses," and the worst—which might be only farmhouses or cottages—served only molasses. Many inns were run by farmers as a secondary source of income, and their casual attitudes towards guests were likely to outrage visitors from abroad.

"sinewy hens and hard bacon"

Equally outrageous to well-heeled tourists was the fact that you could not get a gourmet meal at an inn, no matter how much you paid. Visitors and newly-arrived settlers joined in denouncing Canadian food; but, for the British, there was some satisfaction in this. It had long been fashionable for everyone to sneer at British cookery. "Heaven keep every Christian from their gravies," Heine had warned, and Sydney Smith had denounced their entrées as "barbarian Stonehenge masses of meat." How delicious, therefore, to be able to travel to Canada, where the cooking was even worse! Commentators outdid themselves in reviling the food served in Canadian inns. In Nova Scotia, according to a Captain Moorsom, you would get "sinewy hens and hard bacon." Anna Jameson describes the breakfast served to her at a country inn by an attentive landlady: "She got out her best tea, kept for her own drinking (which tasted for all the world, like musty hay), and buttered toast, i.e. fried bread steeped in melted butter, and fruit preserved in molasses." Susanna Moodie's lugubrious friend Tom Wilson complains of his diet at an inn in the "bush": "Pork, morning, noon, and night, swimming in its own grease!. . . and that disgusting specimen of unleavened bread, yclept cakes in the pan." Apparently pancake-making had not yet become an art.

But these reflections were made by upper-and middle-class travellers. Others saw things quite differently. For some, even "sinewy hens and hard bacon" were recognized as luxuries, something they wouldn't have had in Europe. William Thompson, a textile worker originally from Aberdeen who financed his travels by stopping here and there to work as a mill-hand, found the productivity of the soil more interesting than the view of Niagara from below; for him, the word "beautiful" was likely to mean "fertile." The poor settlers—"a class of farmers different from those that use silver spoons"—were to be evaluated not in terms of their quaintness but by whether they had bettered their condition by emigrating, and if so, how. His criteria for a successful landscape – tidy farms, kitchens hung with bacon and beef, fine horses, fat cows—would have been accounted dull by the seekers after the picturesque.

"Rambles"

It took an unusual man to combine both viewpoints, the picturesque and the practical. Joe Howe called his travel sketches "Rambles," but the hard slogging he'd put in to compose them was not so casual as the title suggests. He'd bought his own newspaper, *The Novascotian*, at the age of twenty-three, going into debt to do so. Now in 1827 he had a wife and family to support and a newspaper to run, and, in those times of depression, many Nova Scotians had land and buildings

Horse-Power

Few Canadians or Maritimers went a day without going somewhere behind the backside of a horse. Winter and summer, on roads, farms and water, horses worked in trade, transportation and construction for backwoods pioneers and city-folk alike. The blacksmith's shops and stables were the service stations then.

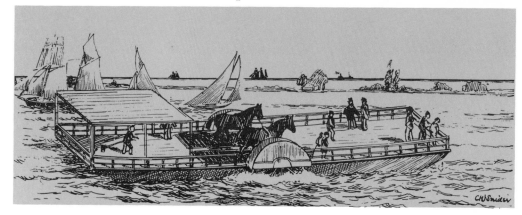

Horse boats, powered by horse-driven treadmills, were attempted as ferrys over short distances.

Before steam railways, horses were used to haul carriages along wooden tracks topped with iron.

**David Douglas
The B.C. Botanist**

A few of his monuments stand today as he described them in 1825: "the most striking and graceful objects in nature" – the *Douglas* firs of B.C. This energetic botanist was the son of a Scottish stonemason. He had no patience with school and left at age 12. He preferred to be outdoors, collecting plants and animals, and his interest led to a commission in 1823 to collect plants in the U.S. and on the West coast. His journeys were made mostly on foot: one such trek, Fort Vancouver to Fort St. James, in 1827, was over 1,150 *miles*. His remarkably detailed work led to the introduction of 215 new species of plants to botany textbooks, and the *Douglas* fir takes its name at the top of the catalogue. At age 35, *en route* home from Siberia, he was gored to death by a bull in Hawaii.

but no hard cash. Howe travelled all over the province, by stage, on horseback and on foot, trying to collect the subscription money owed him. On these experiences he based a series of articles which he published in his newspaper. Howe's "Rambles" were not only popular; they changed the way Nova Scotians felt about their country, and consequently the way they acted.

Howe was no stranger to the cult of the picturesque. He'd educated himself on the Romantic poets and knew the finer points of rugged scenery, sylvan beauties, seashores and thunderstorms as well as anyone. And he was not above writing in the same vein: the "Rambles" contain passages as purple as might be wished, with flourishes of adjectives of which Scott himself might have approved. If you wanted your feeling bosom fired, Howe could point out enough things in Nova Scotia capable of firing it. He lavished as much attention on a descent into the coal mine near Pictou and on the number of grist-mills in a county as he did on more conventional scenery. He took care to describe each town and village he visited –

and he praised the cooking in the inns!

Before Howe, Nova Scotians lived in isolated communities of differing racial backgrounds; many never travelled, and most knew little about their neighbours. Through Howe, they came to see their country as a whole. Before Howe, patriotism meant loyalty to Britain, after Howe, it meant loyalty to Nova Scotia as well. Howe was familiar with the colonial mentality, the belief that all things good flowed from across the ocean, that everything in Nova Scotia was second-rate; that was the fashionable opinion among the fashionable people of Halifax. He wanted to convince his countrymen "that there really is something in their own country worth going to see" and that sentiments of love and pride for their land were desirable. "Indulge the feeling, man," he told them, "don't be ashamed of it; for t'is a tower of strength to the country." And he succeeded. He won his later fight for responsible government partly because he had convinced the people, through a series of newspaper travel sketches, that their land was worth governing.

Winter was the best time to travel overland in the colonies. Cutters could skim over the icy surface of a road that had been a muddy quagmire six months earlier. Farmers waited until winter to transport many of their crops to market.

Queen Victoria

Princess Alexandrina Victoria became Queen, at age 18, in 1837, but it was a long time before her colonists discovered that they had become Victorians. News sometimes took two months to cross the Atlantic. But in good time the English settlers got around to celebrating.

ORDER OF THE PROCESSION,

ON PROCLAIMING HER MAJESTY QUEEN VICTORIA.

MARSHALL.

High Constable, on Horseback, with his Baton

Three Constables—mounted, with Staves.

Four Pioneers—with Axes.

BAND.

One Company 24th Regiment, as Guard.

Sheriff's Officers—mounted.

Trumpeter, mounted. } Sheriff—in Carriage. { *Trumpeter, mounted.*

High Bailiff—mounted.

City Constables—mounted.

Councilmen—in Carriages.

Aldermen—in Carriages.

Trumpeter, mounted. } Mayor—in Carriage. { *Trumpeter, mounted.*

City Clerk, and Chamberlain—in Carriage.

Militia Officers—mounted.

Private Gentlemen on Horseback, or in Carriages.

Members of the Bar, in their Robes.

District Magistrates, in Carriages.

Heads of Departments, in Carriages

Members of the Assembly.

Members of the Legislative Council

Members of the Executive Council.

Inhabitants—on Foot

Near the front of the coronation parade, "Four Pioneers—with Axes," represented the young colonies.

The young Queen's quip "I shall be good" helped set the moral tone of the Victorian era. The strict prudery and social conventions that developed eventually spilled into colonial life.

"Fashionable Canadians"

"Chaste and elegant" dresses were worn to balls, according to the papers.
In garrison towns, the big social *fêtes* brought out all the military regalia —
colourful outfits compared with the blue and black civvies in vogue for men.

Richard Levinge painted this group setting out for an excursion in New Brunswick. The ladies wore so many wraps they were nicknamed "muffins."

An officer of the British army and a Quebec merchant are drawn in winter dress.

This fashionable habitant couple dons straw for the hot summer months.

79

Archibald MacNab, clan chief, fancied himself the regal laird of his Ottawa Valley colony. But the portrait colours over a tyrannical, gambling, money-hungry thorn in the side of his kinsmen. Despite his avarice, he died in poverty.

CHAPTER SEVEN

Feudal Domains

It is a grand country for the rich speculator who can afford to lay out a large sum. . . .

Catherine Parr Traill, *The Backwoods of Canada,* 1836

Every winter during the twenties and thirties, the citizens of York watched for a strange but familiar sight: an old man, dressed in a shabby sheepskin coat with the fur still on and a sheepskin hat with the tail wound round his neck as a muffler. This apparition would drive into town on a large box sleigh, up to his elbows in buffalo robes. Under the robes, as everyone knew, was a pair of singular sheepskin boots, pulled on over a pair of regular boots. There was nothing unusual about this in itself. The clothes of backwoodsmen, made out of whatever they had, were always irregular. Many working-class settlers wore sheepskin coats and hats instead of the sleek fur topcoats or four-caped tweed overcoats and beaver hats worn by more affluent men, and many drove the rough and clumsy box sleighs instead of the smaller cutters with their curving lines and bright ornaments used for pleasure outings. But later in the day the same sleigh, with the same seedy driver, would be seen with one of the most fashionable ladies in York tucked in under the buffalo robes; Lady Sarah Maitland, for instance, or some other member of the vice-regal train. The driver was the famous Colonel Talbot, the hermit of Lake Erie, founder of the Talbot settlement and owner of 65,000 acres of choice land.

The Colonel was noted for his peculiar attitudes towards dress. "The best coats," he had once said, "are on the backs of stupid fops, broken-down merchants, and clerks with beggarly salaries" and "the heaviest gold chain dangles from the fob of gamblers and blacklegs." Colonel Talbot had no intention of being confused with such trash. He was proud of the homespun made in Port Talbot, and had been known to attend a formal ball in a homespun suit of red and blue check, which must have stood out among the military uniforms and crinolined ballgowns. But it was his privilege to dress as he chose.

In fact, people would have been disappointed if the Colonel had given up his sheepskins and crude homespuns. He was already a bit of a legend, and well-bred English visitors often went out of their way to visit him. His house, Castle Malahide, was like the clothes of its owner: scruffy on the outside, but with hidden elegance. Around the yard were various sheds and outbuildings, haphazardly arranged, in which the Colonel kept his "innumerable" geese and chickens. One of these was the original log shanty in which he had lived when he first settled the area at the turn of the century, back in the days when he had occasionally eaten porcupine and had done his own boot-cleaning, washing, churning and bread-making, in addi-

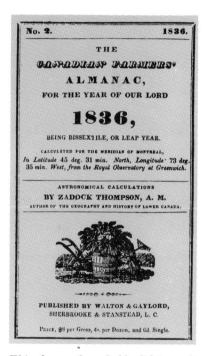

This almanack probably didn't predict that 1836 would be a year of crop failure and financial panic across the entire North American continent.

Thomas Talbot
The Curious Colonel of Malahide

Thomas Talbot was quite the ladies' man! Rumour has it he had fallen in love with a member of the Royalty – far above his station – and that was why he had sold his commission and settled in Canada in 1801. Eccentric though he was in his private and his public life, his habits and his dress, he was a "plain dealer." In 1804 he was granted 5,000 acres of land on Lake Erie; by 1831 he controlled 65,000 acres from Niagara to Detroit. He had built the roads, attracted the region's 6,000 colonists, kept the peace, maintained the law (as he saw fit), kept the accounts of mortgages and sales, and defied all authority and intervention from outsiders. He entertained few visitors at his home, "Castle Malahide," and let it be known to one, Anna Jameson (see page 45), that he hadn't seen anyone for sixteen years besides servants. When he died in 1853, at age 82, he was not loved, but he was a legend.

tion to cooking for the twenty woodsmen working for him.

His larger house was built in 1833. You entered the main building by crossing the porch, where there would be more chickens, "sundry implements of husbandry," and perhaps the dead bobcat, "ghastly and horrible," which Anna Jameson saw there during her visit to the Colonel in 1837. The front door led to a vestibule where the Colonel kept his chicken feed and the occasional stray chicken, his barrels of flour, his sheepskins, saddle and bridle, and anything else he wanted handy to the door. The next room was a kind of study, where the Colonel did business and entertained guests. Its walls were of unplastered logs, and it contained only practical furniture: a pine table, a few chairs with leather or rush seats, a bookcase, and a desk. The kitchen was large, with a huge fireplace and a table for the servants and workmen. The "company" end of the house contained the dining room, which at one stage had red wallpaper and gold moulding, and several bedrooms. The best one, where Anna Jameson slept, had crimson velvet wallpaper, a "Turkey carpet," and equally civilized furniture. The cellar was used for storing the usual root vegetables and milk and the unusual quantities of wine and liquor the Colonel kept on hand. The servants slept in the four-room attic. This motley establishment overlooked Lake Erie, and behind it stretched the Colonel's personal six-hundred-acre farm.

"Gay Tom Talbot"

No one could imagine why such a man, descendant of the ancient Talbots of Castle Malahide in Ireland, once so familiar with Court and social life that he was known as "Gay Tom Talbot," would have thrown up the brilliant army career that was supposed to lie ahead of him and exile himself to Upper Canada to chop down trees.

Some thought it was thwarted love, others thwarted ambition. It may have been that Talbot wished to establish a dynasty in Canada equal to the one in Ireland. He told Mrs. Jameson jokingly that he was "the grand autocrat of the forests," but in fact he believed it.

disputes over land

"On leaving my apartment in the morning," Mrs. Jameson says, "I used to find strange groups of figures lounging round the door, ragged, black-bearded, gaunt, travel-worn and toil-worn emigrants, Irish, Scotch, and American, come to offer themselves as settlers." Talbot called them "land pirates." Although he was technically a government land-agent, in charge of overseeing settlement, Talbot was not fond of giving out land. No one was allowed to settle in his immediate vicinity, and he made things as difficult as possible for those who wanted to settle in Dunwich and Aldborough, the two townships he considered "his." He placed families at inconvenient distances from one another and refused to develop good roads for them. He could do this easily because, by a curious arrangement with the British Colonial Office, Talbot himself got one hundred and fifty acres for every fifty he doled out to a settler in these townships. If he didn't like the look of a man, he located him in a swamp.

He would only interview applicants before noon, since he liked to devote the afternoons to drinking. He had once heard that a man who was drunk before noon would die a drunkard, so he was scrupulous in his observance of the time. The interviews were conducted through Talbot's famous sliding window. Ever since one large irate settler had pinned the rather short Colonel to the ground and refused to let him up until he granted a good piece of land, the Colonel kept a solid wall between himself and his prospects. If there was any trouble, the Colonel would close the window and order his manservant to set on the dogs.

Talbot was constantly embroiled in disputes over land. Though the settlers he supervised outside the two original townships were happy enough, those in Dunwich and Aldborough had a bad habit of petitioning. They wanted two hundred acres instead of fifty, they felt the Colonel's personal 65,000 acres had been obtained at their expense, and they demanded roads. And, once the Talbot Settlement was underway, members of the Family Compact wanted a piece of the action. They intimated that they wouldn't mind a few estates for themselves, but the Colonel wasn't giving. "I'll be d____d if you get one foot of land here," he told them. Whenever harassment from either side became too severe, Talbot was off to England, for he had obtained his original grant through personal influence: he had once been Governor Simcoe's Aide-de-Camp, he'd gone to school with the Duke of Wellington, and he knew one of the King's sons. After each of these visits he returned either with an enlarged grant or a confirmation of his powers, and could thumb his nose at the settlers and the York government alike

a Tory of the old school

He was a Tory of the old school; of a school so old, in fact, that it hardly existed any more. Mrs. Jameson found him rather sad. "He had passed his life in worse than solitude. He will admit of no equal in the vicinity. His only intercourse has been with inferiors and dependents, whose servility he despised, and whose resistance enraged him – men whose interest rested on his favour – on his will, from which there was no appeal. Hence despotic habits, and contempt even for those he benefitted ... all the disadvantages, in short, of royalty, only on a smaller scale." The Colonel himself told her, "I would not, if any one was to offer me the uni-

The forest had been pushed back to make room for Fergus, U.C. (above) just a few years before this 1837 sketch was made. Kingston (below) is shown in 1824, 150 years after Frontenac raised the first stockade roofbeam on the site. Yet the forest crowds in around both settlements, and the tree stumps remind the citizens of the back-breaking work needed to expand the town limits.

Milltown

Milltowns, especially with flour mills, were centres of pioneer life. After each harvest settlers would trek, paddle, or pole to the mill with their crop, leave one-twelfth with the miller as payment, then lug the finished flour home. To avoid round-trips of many days, it was important to live either in or near a milltown. In some cases the mills went up before settlement, on the safe bet that settlement would soon follow. Sawmills also followed settlements closely, and, depending on the local crop, so did oatmeal, barley, carding and paper mills.

This picture of a sawmill at Stanley, N.B., is one of a series drawn to attract emigrants to the company-owned town. Mills were a town's first industry.

verse, go through again the *horrors* I have undergone in forming this settlement." He added hastily that he did not repent it: he had just as much scorn for the follies of civilized life as he had for the crudeness of the settlers.

But his greatest hatred was reserved for teetotallers, "damned cold water drinking societies," and Reformers, who were often the same people. The former threatened his famous cellar, the latter his privileges. When Reform first appeared, he voiced approval when "his people" formed themselves into gangs armed with clubs and went around breaking up meetings and breaking heads. In 1833 he wrote, "My *Rebels* endeavoured to hold a meeting at St. Thomas on the 17th, . . . in which they were frustrated by my Loyal Guards, who routed the rascals at all points and drove them out of the village like sheep, numbers with broken heads leaving their hats behind them – the glorious work of old Colonel Hickory. In short it was a most splendid victory."

another self-exiled aristocrat

But in this, as in everything, time was against him, and in the end it was all for nothing. He never married and had no heir to whom he could leave his vast estate. A nephew who tried out for the position found the life so dull he returned to Ireland. Another nephew altered the Colonel's house in his absence, transforming it into a vision of English country-house splendour and banishing the chickens, and the Colonel never forgave him. He left Castle Malahide, lonely, bitter, and appalled by the creeping radicalism he saw all around him. He had come to Canada to live in the past, but even in Canada the past could not go on forever.

Talbot's eccentricities, Tory beliefs, and self-destructive pride were not unique. Neither were his squabbles with his settlers. But, unlike another

self-exiled aristocrat, he was not an outright cheat.

Even his enemies agreed that Archibald MacNab of MacNab, seventeenth chief of the clan, was "imposing and noble" in appearance, chivalrous and polite in manner, and hospitable to strangers. He had a certain "manly beauty," doubtless inherited from his uncle, the sixteenth chief, who had fathered thirty-two illegitimate children. In full Highland rig, with his own family piper in attendance, he must have appeared like a mirage to the poor Scottish emigrants he was in the habit of meeting at the Montreal wharves. They would have been flattered to have been invited by such a man to share in the glories of "his township." In any case, he had little difficulty in persuading many of them to set their marks to an agreement with him whereby they became virtual serfs, sworn to pay him a bushel of wheat per cleared acre per year and thereby bound to him and his family forever. In fact, the land was not his; the settlers were supposed to own the land once they had performed their settlement duties. But MacNab had his mind set on establishing a highland clan in Canada, and he was able to impose on both the government and the settlers themselves for twenty years.

not just any MacNab

MacNab was not just any MacNab. He was *the* MacNab, as he would remind any unfortunate soul who dared to call him "Mister." Behind him were a thousand years of history. The MacNabs had fought on the side of Bonnie Prince Charlie, lost the major part of their property and gambled away the rest, and it was these fallen fortunes the MacNab was attempting to restore by bleeding the settlers in Upper Canada. High society in Montreal and Toronto, where the novels of Sir Walter Scott were at the height of their popularity (and it was MacNab's ancestor, it was whispered, who

The implacable gaze from the crest of the clan MacNab is a stark reminder of the iron-fisted feudal rule enforced by Archibald MacNab in his Renfrew County domain. If any of his settlers had any question about who was their laird, The MacNab's own stoney gaze set the matter straight in no time.

John Rolph
A Citizen Above Suspicion

He must have been a convincing liar, for in the atmosphere of suspicion that surrounded the troubles in '37, John Rolph had the ear of Governor Bond Head while planning the tactics of the rebels. He was both a lawyer and doctor by training, but quit his law practice after a row over a case with a judge. In 1831 he began his medical practice in York, teaching medicine on the side. He sat with the Reform Party in the U.C. Assembly, and in 1836 was appointed to Council by the governor. As tensions between the Tories and their critics worsened, Rolph became involved with the plans and strategies for the *coup d'état*. He was a respectable doctor, only a Reformer, a citizen above suspicion. But on the eve of revolt, his double-dealing was found out and he fled to the U.S. In 1843, with amnesty, he returned to Canada, started a medical school and became one of the founders of the liberal "Clear Grit" Party.

had been the model for the hero of *Waverley*), found this goal both romantic and praiseworthy, and the MacNab was feasted and fêted, aided and abetted wherever he went. He did not mention to Sir Peregrine Maitland, Sir Francis Bond Head and the others with whom he became intimate that the latest cause of the decline of the MacNab fortunes was himself. Following in his uncle's footsteps, he had run through eighty thousand pounds in one year of gambling, high living and wild oats in Paris.

clan loyalty

The settlers he enticed to his wilderness on the banks of the Madawaska River in the Ottawa Valley did not have powerful friends. Most of them could not read. Many, though not all, were from Scotland, victims of the Clearances, poor cotters with a long tradition of clan loyalty and unquestioning obedience to their Chief. It did not occur to them to doubt that the land they were breaking their backs on was not the Laird's, that his word was not law, that his exactions were not his due. He had not fulfilled his promise of seeing them safely transported and of providing them with a year's supplies to get them started. No matter: if the Laird could not afford to send them by boat, they would walk, for twenty-eight days, through swamps and forests. If he could not afford to give them grain, they would eat potatoes. They dutifully asked his permission to leave the township to obtain work, which numbers were forced to do, since their poor land would not support their families. They had expected cleared farmland, and they were confronted with acres of trees which they themselves had to cut down. Few were experienced with axes; they stood in washtubs while chopping, to avoid cutting their feet. It was curious that the Laird sold the timber and kept the money for himself; it wasn't done that way in the

neighbouring townships. If any complained, the Laird was at hand to tell them how grateful they should be.

Increasingly, some did complain. To those willing to play the part of old family retainers, MacNab was generous and protective, but to those who dared to oppose him in any way he was merciless. He construed any murmur against himself as high treason, both to the King and to God, for was he not a chief by divine right? He did not go so far as to execute his enemies; even the Family Compact would not tolerate this. Instead, he used his power as a magistrate to persecute them through the law. He held peculiar trials, at which he acted as judge, jury, plaintiff, and chief witness. To some, he refused permission to leave the township, thus giving them the choice between starving to death or disobeying his orders. If they disobeyed, he tried to throw them into jail for debt. If any of the other settlers assisted those whom he called his "black sheep," they too became black sheep and subject to the same treatment.

"black sheep"

The confrontation between MacNab and his supposed clansmen soon became an underground war. MacNab played the part of dinosaur, huge and powerful but too stupid to change. The settlers could not openly oppose him: he had the government on his side, and the petitions they managed to send, with the aid of the few among them who could read and write, were ignored. But from the old days in Scotland they'd learned how to dodge and hide, and they took to evading MacNab's process-servers. No stranger could enter the Flat Rapids settlement where the "black sheep" were concentrated without being greeted by a chorus of ox-horns and small-arms fire. At this warning, every male inhabitant headed for the bush and stayed there till the coast was clear.

In the spring of 1837, the MacNab still reigned supreme in his large log castle. But history was against him. When the news of Mackenzie's uprising reached him, he wrote a pompous letter to Sir Francis Bond Head:

My Dear Sir Francis:

The spirit of my fathers has been infused into my soul by recent events, and has roused within me the recollection and memory of the prestige of my race. The only Highland Chieftain in America offers himself, his clan, and the MacNab Highlanders, to march forward in the defence of the country—
"Their swords are a thousand, their hearts are but one."

We are ready to march at any moment.—Command my services at once, and we will not leave the field till we have routed the hell-born rebels, or
"In death be laid low,
With our backs to the field, and our face to the foe."

I am yours sincerely,
MacNab.

Everything about this letter is characteristic: the exalted diction, the quotations from Scott, the consciousness of position, and especially the supreme assurance with which MacNab speaks for men whom he considered "his." He was living a dream, inspired by history and novels. But to his humiliation, when he mustered his forces, only two men volunteered to go to the front. The rest were afraid to serve under him. They'd seen what he could do with civil law, and under martial law he would have the power of life and death over them.

If MacNab had played his cards differently from the beginning, he might have succeeded in making his fortune and restoring the Clan MacNab in Scotland. But the forces of democracy were too strong for him. By now the settlers had

Francis Bond Head was sent as governor to Upper Canada with instructions to conciliate political opinion in the province. Instead he acted like a feudal overlord, reactionary in the extreme instead of flexible, and infuriated responsible Tories and Reformers. London recalled him in 1838.

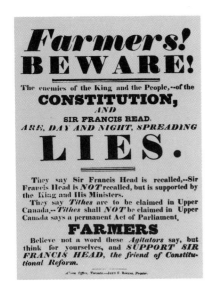

*Governor Francis Bond Head took
to posters and speeches pinning
the unrest in Upper Canada on
"reformers and republicans."
He made British patriotism the
issue, cleverly sidestepping the
growing criticism of his politics
and the colony's restlessness.*

learned more about their rights, and when
"Radical Jack" Durham came to power they
finally had someone who would listen to them. An
investigator was sent to MacNab Township and
the extent to which MacNab had bent the law to
suit his own ends was exposed. The members of
the Family Compact turned up their noses when
facts they must have privately suspected were
made public. Even worse, the settlers now learned
for the first time that their land did not belong to
MacNab. He was merely a land-agent like any
other, and as they had long since fulfilled their settlement duties, the land was not his but theirs.
MacNab's power over them was gone, and he left
the country a ruined man.

Not all large land-agents were bad land-agents.
It was possible for the system to work, more or
less, if the agent was honest and had a real interest
in the welfare of those he was supervising. Peter
Robinson's settlement of poor Irish in Peterborough County, for instance, was a relative success.
Each family was given, by the government, a hundred acres of land, with another hundred for every
grown son. Each family also received a cow, an
axe, an auger, a hand-saw, a hundred nails, two
gimlets, three hoes, a kettle, a frying pan, an iron
pot, and enough seed-potatoes and seed-corn to
put in a crop. In addition to all these implements—
some of which the settlers would never have seen
before and wouldn't have known how to use—each
family was given a log shanty, erected at government expense for ten dollars, and daily rations of
pork and flour for a year and a half. This was
hardly lavish, but the government was criticised by
some for doing too much. At first there was a certain amount of trading—the gimlets and augers
were exchanged for cheap whisky—but most families settled in, cleared their land, and began churning out crops and livestock. Mr. Robinson was
popular with the settlers. "The manner in which
they met him was quite affecting," one observer reported. "It was more to bless him as a benefactor
than to receive him as a visitor."

But the system was often stacked against the
settler. The land-agent had connections, the settler
had none. Often he was ignorant of the terms on
which the land-agent had obtained the grant in the
first place, and might clear his ten acres only to
find that, due to some confusion in deed convey-
ance, or other shady dealing, it really belonged to
someone else. If he didn't fulfill his settlement
duties to the land-agent's satisfaction, he could
simply be kicked out, with no compensation. Pro-
testing was dangerous, since the land-agent was
frequently the local magistrate. If he went to a
higher authority—the provincial government, for
instance—he would find that few would take his
word against that of a member of the "better"
class. In the world of these well-born land-agents,
old school ties prevailed.

Like dinosaurs, the aristocratic old land-bar-
ons devoured all they could get. Like dinosaurs,
they died out because they could not adapt themselves to changing times. And like dinosaurs, they
were seen by those who followed them as quaint
and slightly tragic only when they were gone.

Money

Money was a scarce commodity in Britain's North American colonies. Barter and long-term credit were the common basis of trade. Coins in circulation came from all over the world and were given different values from Halifax to York, which caused endless confusion. Spanish dollars (pistareens) were used widely in the Maritimes; in P.E.I. holes were punched through them ("holey dollars") so they couldn't be used off the Island. Old U.S. coinage was dumped north of the border, and "army bills," a form of promissory note introduced during the War of 1812, accustomed people to safe paper money. Anchor money, coins with an anchor motif, was struck in 1822 for British colonies generally. Nova Scotia's government notes and the sou tokens of Lower Canada's banks and merchants added to the variety. But all in all, barter was probably still the only easy way out of the money jungle.

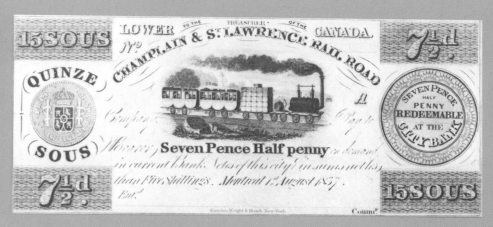

Although some notes were shillings and pence, Canadians counted in America's dollars and cents.

Bank notes issued by chartered banks were often redeemable only at a formidable surcharge.

Two tokens of exchange from the period, of dubious value.

The Bank of Upper Canada, a child of the Family Compact, was the first bank in the province.

All in the Family

In Toronto society, the Robinson family was considered the *crème de la crème*. Not only was the father the Chief Justice of Upper Canada, but his wife and he were blessed with four daughters and four sons. However, the term "family" had other meanings in U.C. in the era. Rich and influential families, often related through the marriages of their children, were seen by working people and farmers as a privileged "Compact" who controlled the courts, banks, business and government.

George Theodore Berthon's The Three Robinson Sisters—*high society fashion.*

Emma Robinson and daughter, Mary. All the girls married within the Compact.

Berthon's portrait of John Beverley Robinson immortalized both the Chief Justice and the artist. As "court painter" for the city's elite, Berthon, whose father had been an artist for Napoleon, painted 29 portraits in a single year for $1710—an astounding income for the day.

Louis-Joseph Papineau's powerful oratory inspired some French-Canadians to call him their messiah. He called himself a philosophical rebel and guided reformers in L.C.'s Assembly; but when violence broke out he fled to the U.S.

William Lyon Mackenzie, editor of the Colonial Advocate *and first mayor of Toronto, led the radicals in Upper Canada. When the fighting began near Montgomery's Tavern, it became obvious his pen was mightier than his sword.*

CHAPTER EIGHT

Honourable Men

We have to inquire if we have not reached the period in which the first authority of the state should recover the respect it has lost. . . .

Louis-Joseph Papineau, *The Ninety-Two Resolutions,* 1834

Dr. William "Tyger" Dunlop was a well-known character, not only in Upper Canada but throughout the English-speaking world. He had first come to the colonies to serve as a medical officer during the War of 1812. After that he had travelled widely, earning his nickname by shooting tigers in India. He had been a newspaper editor and a member of the Edinburgh wits, and had acquired a reputation for his "grotesque manner" and his habit of practical joking. He was shaggy-haired and enormous–one friend described him as "a compound of a bear and a gentleman"–and as eccentric in his dress as Colonel Talbot, his good friend. He had introduced himself to Talbot in typical Tyger style, pausing in the woods outside Castle Malahide to turn his coat and hat inside out, then shambling up to the door, roaring. "Let him in, Geoffrey," the Colonel is reported to have said to his manservant. "It's either the Devil or Dr. Dunlop."

Dunlop's comfortable house, built of logs but with a brass doorplate, had a huge dining room with a round mahogany table for twelve, and his enormous liquor stand had space for twelve one-gallon bottles. Dunlop named these "The Twelve Apostles," implying that the true gospel was to be found within them. "Though Toryism were expelled from all the rest of the globe," said his Edinburgh crony Maginn, "it would find shelter in the log-house of Dunlop."

Dr. Dunlop was indeed a Tory. His Toryism had a theory behind it: he felt that a single ruler, such as a lieutenant-governor, could be held responsible for his actions, whereas a number of men, such as an elected Assembly, could not. "Responsible government," he once said, was "a trap by knaves to catch fools." He appeared before William Lyon Mackenzie's Special Committee of Grievances in 1835, but gave them cold comfort.

Pray sir, said McK [sic] would you not recommend that the Crown Lands, should be placed under the management of the Colonial Legislature? Certainly not – And why not sir? – Because you have already a great deal more to do than is properly attended to!

In his view, if one man could be stupid, dishonest, irresponsible and incompetent, the evil would only be multiplied by forty if forty men replaced him.

Yet Dunlop was neither a knave nor a fool. He was respected by his farmer neighbours, who often looked to him for advice and leadership, and he was by no means insensible to their mounting discontent and to the legitimate reasons for it. He had come to Upper Canada as an official of the Can-

This cartoon takes a sarcastic swipe at radicals and reformers across Upper Canada. The Tories used every means to discredit their opponents and won the election hands down.

**William Dunlop
"The Tyger"**

He was a born joker with a taste for whiskey and a touch of snuff. After serving as a surgeon in Canada in the War of 1812, he went with his regiment to India, where he earned his nickname in a mad scheme to rid the island of Saugor of tigers by subduing the beasts with snuff. He returned to his native Scotland in 1820 and spent the next five years living a bohemian life in London and Edinburgh, teaching medicine and writing. In 1826 John Galt of the Canada Company persuaded him to join the company in colonizing the vast Huron Tract in U.C., and Dunlop made the journey once more to Canada. He immediately applied his energies, and his wit, to the job: unlike the hundred other books written as guides for emigrants, his *Statistical Sketches* (1832) are a collage of practical information and lively anecdote. The Tyger never married, and lived most of his life in Goderich on Lake Erie.

ada Company, a vast English land-holding company which had purchased the Huron Tract with an eye to partially settling it and then disposing of the rest of its million acres at profits of up to 500 percent. Dunlop had been "Warden of the Forests" and general supervisor, and though he had undertaken this job out of his usual perversity and boyish sense of adventure, he had stayed to settle in. The affairs of the country and the Company were now his main concern, and he knew that there was something wrong with both. But though he agreed with William Lyon Mackenzie about the evils, he did not agree on the remedy.

grievance-collecting and rabble-rousing

Other Tories, either more knavish or more foolish than Dunlop, blamed the growing discontent on that scoundrel Mackenzie. It was stupid, though, for the young Tory bloods back in 1826, to have broken into his house with only his old mother home to defend it, smashed his printing press and thrown it into Lake Ontario. His paper, the *Colonial Advocate*, had been failing then, but the incident, the publicity, and the damages Mackenzie got when he sued, had given the "rascal" and the paper new life. Mackenzie had been a gadfly ever since, poking his nose in where it was not wanted, grievance-collecting and rabble-rousing. What business was it of his which members of the "Family Compact," as he called them, were married to which other members' sisters, cousins and aunts? Surely it must have been obvious to anyone that there was only a limited number of women in *good* society in Upper Canada, and one had to marry somebody. Why should he care that many of them had large tracts of land that they were leaving undeveloped, hoping for a later rise in prices? If farmers were isolated from each other and the development of rural communities was retarded, that was too bad, but what sensible man

with land would sell it cheap when he could get more for it later? Of course the Family Compact kept official positions and the decision-making powers in their own hands: anyone could see that they were the only ones educated enough to govern properly.

And as for education, why were the farmers clamouring for it? What would they or their children *do* with it? The Compact was quite satisfied with the educational facilities that already existed. There was Upper Canada College, for instance, where they sent their sons. It didn't bother them that critics sneeringly called it the "Prepare-a-Tory school." They were not ashamed of the label. The English officials sent out from time to time couldn't agree with them more: public education, at public expense, for the sons of farmers, was ridiculous. "What do you need such schools for?" one of them wrote. "There will always be enough well-educated Old Countrymen to transact all public business, and we can leave Canadians to clean up the bush." They were accused of having the ear of the lieutenant-governor, but who else was the poor man supposed to have dinner with? You could not very well ask him to dine with low people such as printers and blacksmiths.

"a petty colonial oligarchy"

The Tories were not only angered by Mackenzie's attacks, they were confused. What did these farmers have to complain about? Many of them had done much better than they would have back in Europe. Why couldn't they just accept the customs of Upper Canada, one of which was that the "best people" had control? They were not British aristocrats, although there had been some talk of creating a Canadian peerage. By and large, they were simply the ones who had got there first. They had made their fortunes as merchants, middlemen, peddling goods to the farmers at high prices and selling the farmers' produce, keeping, of course, a goodly chunk of the profit. But being a merchant was still socially ambiguous, which may have been why the Compact members were so insistent on the subject of their own innate superiority. "We have here," said the sharp-tongued Mrs. Jameson, "a petty colonial oligarchy, a self-constituted aristocracy, based upon nothing real, nor even upon any thing imaginary; and we have all the mutual jealousy and fear, and petty gossip, and mutual meddling and mean rivalship, which are common in a small society."

vicious journalism

Mackenzie was fond of pricking the Compact members in their most vulnerable spot, their snobbish vanity. They had gentlemanly pretensions, very well, he would go out of his way to show that their pretensions were unfounded. In his paper he attacked their family connections, their private lives and behaviour, their affectations and their honour. It was an age of vicious journalism, and much of what Mackenzie printed would be instant grounds for libel cases today; but Mackenzie was not alone. The opposition struck back at him through *their* newspapers, even going so far as to sneer at him for supporting his aged mother. No one expected newspapers to be impartial: if you wanted a balanced view, you read the papers of all three factions, the Tories, the Reformers, and the Radicals. Mrs. Jameson saw the Tories as the party of influence and the Reformers as jealous would-be's. The Radicals, she thought, were those who wanted a republic rather than a colony. "At present," she wrote in early 1837, "they are neither influential nor formidable." She also complained of the "base, vulgar, inflammatory party feeling" of the Canadian newspapers, though no one in the Canadas would have found this remarkable. Mackenzie, however, was an acknowledged master

Forty-eight hours by balloon from England to Canada? A British cartoonist pokes a quill at the ignorance and irresponsibility of the colonial administrators. Lord Durham expects an extremely hazardous time in the colonies—"rough place for the old school, you know."

of the gibe, the thrust, the outraged diatribe, and the rough burlesque. The farmers read his paper and laughed. It was good sport to see the Toronto mighty ones brought down a few pegs.

But Mackenzie fumed and grumbled for over ten years before there was a rebellion. Perhaps this was why the Tories weren't expecting one. For all Mackenzie's raging, their positions were still secure. It wasn't as though things had changed. If the farmers didn't like it, why hadn't they revolted before?

One reason was that they hadn't had time. A man busy clearing his first ten acres, trying to make enough to support his family from year to year and to have enough left over to plant the next season's crop, could not afford to get involved in politics. In the early years the population had been small and the farmers isolated. But by the thirties there was a substantial body of men who had fulfilled their settlement duties and owned their own land. They could vote; more importantly, they could support their families and still take time off to vote; and even more importantly, they could actually get to the places where the voting was to be held. Earlier, they had been hampered by poor roads and lack of information. Now, there were forty newspapers published in Upper Canada. Much political information could be exchanged at the local taverns and inns where travellers would relate the news and retail opinions. Political meetings were held at the inns, too, and the great Mackenzie himself toured the country speaking at them. He was a spellbinding orator, peppering his speeches with colloquialisms and jokes, but his speeches were sometimes interrupted. In Galt, a crowd entered carrying an effigy of Mackenzie stuffed with gunpowder. Religious meetings, too, were seedbeds of political feeling, and the Methodist revival meetings were healthy places to discuss Reform and Radical ideas, just as Anglican pulpits were used for Tory propaganda. Isolated

"Wretched place to put a colony!" All the gold braid in the world won't warm the British officer in this cartoon from Lower Canada.

farmers were still common, but there were enough informed and mobile farmers to form a large constituency for Mackenzie. And they weren't like the farmers of Old England, cowed by authority and still believing in some form of Divine Right. The United States, with its republican ideas and recent revolution, wasn't far. Things could change, and men could change them, if they dared.

the cheering, jeering crowd

Their grievances came to a head in 1837 partly because of the depression which had begun in 1836, and partly because of the outcome of the election held that same year. Elections were not the sedate, secretive, sober affairs they are today. They were rowdy at best, and violent free-for-alls were common. Only men who held free title to their land could vote, but this did not prevent any other man from participating in an election as part of the cheering or jeering crowd. In fact, an election was probably one of the most exciting sporting events a man could attend: better than a cock-fight or a bare-knuckles boxing match, even. Liquor flowed freely and was often provided by the candidates themselves. The candidate, in addition to standing drinks, had to harangue the crowd from the hustings, where he could be pelted with dead cats and other unsavoury objects if he was particularly unpopular. There were bands, flags, and uproarious parades after a winner had been declared, and it was customary for a dummy figure to be made of the opposition candidate, which was marched around in a torchlight procession and hanged or tossed into a bonfire.

Sometimes a party had the equivalent of a hired goon squad. The Family Compact had such a group in Toronto, which was on call not only during elections but at all other times as well. Mackenzie was in the habit of standing on a wagon every market day, to make speeches to the farmers. "Perhaps you know," said an eyewitness, "that the Compact had a lot of hangers-on who would do anything they were told for the soup, clothes and stuff that was given them, and we used to call them 'soupets,' like the bits of bread you put in soup to sop it up. As Mackenzie was talking, suddenly the vestry door was thrown open, and out rushed a crowd of soupets, caught hold of the tongue of Mackenzie's waggon, and ran off with him towards the bay. . . . The soupets nearly had him ducked in the bay before the farmers came to their senses."

loyalty versus republicanism

The elections of 1836 were more riotous than usual, partly because the lieutenant-governor, Sir Francis Bond Head, had become active in politics as the real leader of the Conservatives. He tended to smear Reformers as Yankee-loving traitors and made the issue loyalty versus republicanism. The magistrates, who were supposed to keep order, sometimes used their powers to repress Reform violence while turning a blind eye to Tory mobs. In London, Ontario, "a general riot ensued every day that the polls were open . . . an Orange mob . . . commenced beating a number of Liberals who were taken up for dead. . . . The Liberal poll was secured by two clerks who made their escape into the jail for protection and were locked up." There was no such thing as a secret ballot, so Reform voters were easy targets. In this election, the sixty-four voters were threatened with clubs, and the Reform voters were chased away from the polls and beaten up if they were caught. As Tyger Dunlop wrote, an Upper Canadian election "here, as at home, is accompanied with all the noise, confusion, drunkenness, fighting, malice, and evil-speaking and back-biting that becomes a free people in the exercise of their rights."

The Tories won a landslide victory in the 1836 election. The Reformers, and especially the Radicals, were enraged at the way a supposedly impartial governor had used the loyalty issue to stifle political debate. While more moderate Reform leaders gave up in despair, Mackenzie plotted armed resistance out of frustration. If the electoral system had been subverted, he would have to try other means. This decision put many of Mackenzie's followers in an agonizing position. To take up arms against the government meant to take them up against the army and the Queen. "I was a Scotch Radical," said one shepherd, "and would have helped Mackenzie all I could – until he drew the sword. That proved to me he was not constitutional, and I wouldna any such doings." Many shared this view.

a Quaker

One man who must have thought long and hard about the issue was Samuel Lount, who later marched with Mackenzie down Yonge Street. Lount was a Quaker, and as such would have been brought up with pacifist views. He was on reasonable terms with the government, as he had held a position as a surveyor. He was not a farmer, so he was not suffering personally from the Compact's land speculation or the retention of the Clergy Reserves. But as a blacksmith, shoeing the farmers' horses and mending their ploughshares, he would have had ample chance to become familiar with their complaints. From all reports he was universally well-liked – unlike the fiery Mackenzie, who often put people off – and he was of a mild-mannered and peaceable disposition. During the rebellion itself, he was the one who kept Mackenzie from burning down houses, and mollified Tory housewives after Mackenzie had eaten their food and insulted them. He would not have been easily convinced; yet in the late fall of '37, he was forging pikes at his smithy, knowing full well that they

The wretch that would a tyrant own,
And the wretch, his true born brother,
Who would set the mob above the Throne,
May they be hang'd together!

Who will not sing "God save the King,"
Shall hang as high's the steeple;
But while we sing "God save the King,"
We'll ne'er forget the People. BURNS.

Robert Burns would have bristled at this use of his verse in the Upper Canada Almanack *in 1837. Whoever drew the cartoon forgot to string up the tyrant along with the rebels.*

Colonel Robert Moodie is shot dead as he gallops past the rebels to warn Governor Bond Head.

Following the rout by the British militia at Navy Island, the rebels were caricatured as cowards.

were going to be used in a march against the Compact at Toronto.

Mackenzie and his forces had a slight chance of winning their fight, or at least capturing Toronto. At first, circumstances seemed to be on their side. The entire garrison had been emptied and the soldiers sent to Lower Canada to repress the uprising of *patriotes* there. Mackenzie knew he should strike while the troops were away. But precious time was lost debating methods with his fellow Radicals, who at the last moment were seized with a fit of caution. Communications were fouled up, too, and Mackenzie's men dribbled in to the rendezvous at Montgomery's Inn, outside Toronto, ahead of their military leaders, to find confusion among those in charge and inadequate provisions for themselves. While the Radicals milled around wondering what was happening, Sir Francis sat in Toronto, refusing to believe that anyone would have the bad taste to rebel against *him*. But by the time the Radicals were ready to make their move, the Tories were more or less ready also. The *patriotes,* plagued by a similar indecisiveness, had dispersed and fled, and the troops were on the way back. The moment had been lost, and Mackenzie's brave plans ended in tragi-comic skirmishing and an ignominious flight across a ploughed field. The dispatch case he dropped contained enough incriminating evidence to keep the Tories busy chasing Radicals for months.

Some of Mackenzie's men later felt they would have won if only Lount had led them. Mackenzie was a good critic but he was not a very good organizer; as mayor of Toronto during the cholera outbreak of 1834, he had paid more attention to quibbling than to the mounting stack of corpses. Now his relations with his men left something to be desired. "He abused and insulted several of the men without any shadow of cause, and Lount had to go round and pacify them by telling them not to pay any attention to him as he was not responsible for his actions," said one participant. "If we had locked him up. . . and could then have induced Lount to lead us into the city, we should have overturned the government without any fighting worth talking about."

Lount did not lead, and the battle was over almost before it had begun. But, fearing further Radical attacks or even an invasion from the States, Bond Head called out the local militia. William "Tyger" Dunlop immediately leapt into the fray, which appealed enormously to his quixotic nature. His regiment was called the Huron True Blues, the Huron Braves, the Invincibles, or, by those less impressed, the Bloody Useless. Dunlop dressed them in anything he could get – blanket coats with epaulettes, moccasins with spurs – fed them with whatever food he could lay hands on, armed them with pikes, doubled the grog ration whenever he could, and drilled them regularly. He immediately found himself involved in a running battle, not with the Radicals but with the Canada Company, which had fallen down severely in its role as paternalistic patriarch and refused to supply anything or pay anyone. It became clear to Dunlop that the Canada Company's relationship with its settlers was not the two-way street he had supposed but an inequitable arrangement whereby Canadians did the work and Englishmen took the profits. Finally Dunlop resigned, accusing those who withheld his soldiers' pay of "overweening arrogance and the most cruel neglect":

My life and my property are my country's, and I am willing to lay either or both down when my Sovereign may require them, but my honour is inalienably my own, and I cannot submit to be made, as I lately unwittingly have been, the instrument of the most cruel and grinding oppression, to snatch, without remuneration, his pittance from the peasant or the bread from his children's mouths.

Dunlop, whose Toryism had been resistant to the settlers' plight in times of peace, had had his military honour violated by the same system he had rallied to defend. He later became a political opponent of the Canada Company and a champion of responsible government.

Both Tyger Dunlop and Samuel Lount had been made colonels through the Rebellion. Dunlop's command placed him in a position he found untenable, and, though he never became a Radical, he fought the vested land interests in Canada for many years. Lount's command was short-lived. He was active as a leader only until the decisive skirmish on the outskirts of Toronto, and his military career ended on the gallows. Dunlop was about the most attractive specimen of a Tory that Upper Canada had to offer, and Lount, without any of the harshness and bitterness of Mackenzie, was a most appealing Radical. Each acted according to his principles, and each sincerely believed that what he was doing was in the best interests of the ordinary citizen of Upper Canada. If Dunlop and Lount, instead of Francis Bond Head and Mackenzie, had been the spokesmen for their respective factions, the confrontation would have gone differently. And, whatever the outcome, the aftermath would have been far less bloody.

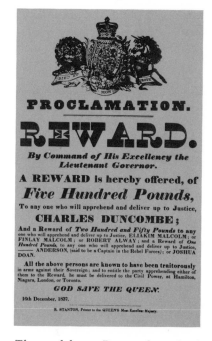

PROCLAMATION.
REWARD.
By Command of His Excellency the Lieutenant Governor.
A REWARD is hereby offered, of Five Hundred Pounds,
To any one who will apprehend and deliver up to Justice,
CHARLES DUNCOMBE;
And a Reward of *Two Hundred and Fifty Pounds* to any one who will apprehend and deliver up to Justice, ELIAKIM MALCOLM; or FINLAY MALCOLM; or ROBERT ALWAY; and a Reward of *One Hundred Pounds*, to any one who will apprehend and deliver up to Justice, ANDERSON, (said to be a Captain in the Rebel Forces); or JOSHUA DOAN.
All the above persons are known to have been traitorously in arms against their Sovereign; and to entitle the party apprehending either of them to the Reward, he must be delivered to the Civil Power, at Hamilton, Niagara, London, or Toronto.
GOD SAVE THE QUEEN.
16th December, 1837.
R. STANTON, Printer to the QUEEN'S Most Excellent Majesty.

The good doctor Duncombe, radical politician, fled with a price on his head to his native California and escaped the hangman's fancy. Unlike some "traitors," he commanded greater respect, and a higher bounty.

CHAPTER NINE

Hunters and Hangings

*Up then, brave Canadians! Get ready your
rifles, and make short work of it . . . our
enemies in Toronto are in terror and dismay—*

William Lyon Mackenzie, 1837

After the fiascos in both Upper and Lower Canada, people might have expected things to quiet down. But more battles were fought, and more blood shed, after the uprisings than during them. And the blood was not all "rebel" blood. Throughout 1838, citizens all along the borders of Upper and Lower Canada – especially outspoken Tories – woke to find their barns and houses blazing. Some were even murdered.

These acts of guerilla warfare were the work of a strange secret society whose trappings make it sound like a cross between the Masons and the Mafia. Members were initiated on their knees, blindfolded. They swore a solemn oath that they would not divulge any of the secrets they were about to learn, and they were threatened with having their throats cut to the bone and their houses burned if they disobeyed. The blindfold was then removed, and swords, pistols and torches were flashed before the initiate's eyes. Several of the disobedient ended up as corpses floating, both piecemeal and intact, down the Detroit River or over Niagara Falls, or in various other streams and estuaries of the northern United States, for the organization had its largest membership base south of the border.

This organization was known as the Patriot Hunters. It had its own secret cipher, its own banking scheme, and a complicated code of knocks and scratches whereby an initiate could get through the door where one of the "Lodges" was being held. It had four degrees of proficiency: the Snowshoe, for beginners; the Beavers; the Grand Masters, and the Patriot Hunters. It had its own flags, embroidered by the members' wives, with a design of an eagle flanked by stars. And it had an elaborate system of signs and signals by which the members could recognize each other. Snowshoes pinched each other's coat sleeves when shaking hands, and when in doubt they stuck their right forefingers in their nostrils or their left ones in their ears. Beavers gnawed their thumbs in imitation of the animal for which they were named, and Patriot Hunters scratched their snuffboxes. The image of hundreds of grown men greeting each other by pinching sleeves, gnawing thumbs or cramming their fingers resolutely up their noses might have caused a neutral observer to underestimate their secret society. But that would have been a mistake: the Hunters were deadly serious. Their aim was to invade and capture Canada, for the purpose of "liberating" it, their rhetoric proclaimed. That there were other motives is indicated by the fact that Loyalist property was to be confiscated and each member of the invading

LOUIS JOSEPH PAPINEAU;
LEADER OF THE REVOLT IN THE CANADA'S.

This silhouette of Papineau appeared in a London newspaper in 1838 with a brief biography noting, "all the energies of his mind have been devoted to an uncompromising hostility of the provincial administration. His integrity of principle is great."

Opposite page: *Troops of the 71st Highland Light Infantry take a load of L.C. rebels off to jail.*

Francois Prieur
The Condemned Idealist

Francois Xavier Prieur was a young merchant in St. Timothée when the revolt broke out in 1837. As leader of the underground *Frères Chasseurs,* he was captured at Beauharnois and sentenced to hang. But his life was spared because of his humane treatment of English hostages, and instead he was sent to the penal colony in Australia. For eight years, together with 58 other rebels, he was confined to a hovel, fed starvation rations, and worked like a slave. Instead of bitterness, his experience planted a deep reverence for life in him, and when he returned to Canada, he turned his energy and concern toward prison reform. By 1875 he was superintendent of all Canadian prisons.

army was to be given rights of plunder and, later, three hundred choice acres. But they genuinely believed that, as soon as they crossed the border, thousands would rush to their side.

the hated British

In Upper Canada, this belief seems to have been largely a delusion. In the few attempts at invasion actually made by the Hunters, the promised support did not materialize, and the invaders were stranded and decimated. But in Lower Canada, where there was a parallel organization known as the Frères Chasseurs, there was widespread underground support for the movement. There were active cells in almost every part of the province; agents crossed the American border and travelled from town to town, returning to the headquarters in Vermont with the names of new members and the money they had collected; and in Montreal a divisional headquarters operated right under the noses of the hated British.

And there was no doubt that the British were hated. For the vast majority of the people of Lower Canada, the hatred had been slow to grow, but it was well rooted. The British had not been exactly welcomed after the Conquest, but neither had they been detested. The Battle of the Plains of Abraham, after all, had been fought by the representatives of two foreign governments, and though the Québecois had swelled the army, they had not been in command. The aristocrats and seigneurs who had sailed back to France after the Conquest had not been in the habit of treating their people so well that their departure was deeply mourned. During the American Revolution and the War of 1812, the French had remained loyal or, at least, indifferent. The Americans, with their Protestantism and levelling cant, were more to be feared than the British, with their King and Anglican Church.

And at first there had been so few British that they scarcely disturbed the rhythms of life in the villages and towns of the Saint Lawrence Valley. There were always the farms, there was always the Church. But gradually the consequences of the British takeover became apparent. The French were not to inherit the empire they had carved out for themselves in the western part of the continent. They were driven back to the Saint Lawrence Valley, and even there they soon felt crowded. Their farms, divided among successive generations of sons, with the soil too exhausted from overcultivation and lack of enrichment, could no longer support their families. And there was little new land available. As in Upper Canada, the huge tracts reserved by the Crown lay vacant. Land speculation flourished, but it was British Tory or Yankee merchants and government officials who were doing the speculating. They alone had the ear of the government and the Colonial Office in London. There was no room at the top for the French.

the patriote movement

There wasn't even much room in the middle. Most of the French-speaking populace could not read. The community was too poor to support a widespread system of schools and too suspicious to accept an English system. But there were a few good schools and colleges, largely Church-run, and a new class of doctors, lawyers and notaries was being built up. However, a young man with ambition could only go so far. Soon he would be stopped by the British hierarchy, barred by his race from ascending further. If he wanted to be a merchant, he would soon find that commerce was controlled by the English. A minority in a country in which they felt themselves disliked, they were a clannish group.

It was the frustrated young professionals who provided the bulk of the leadership for the *patriote*

Un Canadien Errant

Antoine Gérin-Lajoie's books are all but forgotten, but one song he wrote is known by every French and English Canadian: the folk song, *Un Canadien Errant.* He was born and raised in rural Quebec, and as a schoolboy came to accept the traditional belief that the future lay in the land, not in the businesses and professions of the city and town. He was still in his teens when the rebellions of 1837-1838 broke out, but the events left an indelible impression on his work. His 1874 novel, *Jean Rivard,* is a Canadien classic.

Once a Canadian lad,
Exiled from hearth and home,
Wandered, alone and sad,
Through alien lands unknown.
Down by a rushing stream,
Thoughtful and sad one day
He watched the water pass
And to it he did say:

"If you should reach my land,
My most unhappy land,
Please speak to all my friends
So they will understand.
Tell them how much I wish
That I could be once more
In my beloved land
That I will see no more.

"My own beloved land
I'll not forget till death,
And I will speak of her
With my last dying breath.
My own beloved land
I'll not forget till death,
And I will speak of her
With my last dying breath."

Un canadien errant,
Banni des ses foyers,
Un canadien errant,
Banni de ses foyers,
Parcourait en pleurant
Des pays étrangers.
Parcourait en pleurant
Des pays étrangers.

Un jour, triste et pensif,
Assis au bord des flots,
Un jour, triste et pensif,
Assis au bord des flots,
Au courant fugitif
Il adressa ces mots,
Au courant fugitif
Il adressa ces mots:

"Si tu vois mon pays,
Mon pays malheureux,
Si tu vois mon pays,
Mon pays malheureux,
Va, dis à mes amis
Que je me souviens d'eux,
Va, dis à mes amis
Que je me souviens d'eux.

Gérin-Lajoie was 14 when the rebellion occurred. While still in school, he wrote the words to this folk song about a patriote who fled or was banished from his homeland, never to return.

movement of the 1830s. Their idol was Louis-Joseph Papineau. Like Mackenzie, he was a spellbinding orator, and like Mackenzie he had been a member of the elected Assembly. Like Mackenzie, he had railed against Tory privilege as embodied in the Crown-appointed Legislative Council, and had insisted that the government be made responsible to the will of the people. Like Mackenzie, he had admired American republicanism.

poor Scots and Irish

But there were major differences between them. Mackenzie was an active and vituperative critic, but he had proved rather a flop as a member of the legislature and as mayor of Toronto. Papineau, however, shone as a parliamentarian. It was his boast that for over twenty years he had taken the British institution that had been imposed on the French and turned it against the British. Although the hated Legislative Council was composed largely of rich English, the Assembly of Lower Canada was elected. But in 1830 Lower Canada was four-fifths French, so the French dominated the Assembly. And Papineau dominated the French: under his direction, the Assembly had regularly refused to vote funds for projects such as canal systems and roads that the British merchants saw as essential to their expansion and prosperity. Under British rule the French could not seize control of their own destinies, but at least they could block, obstruct and veto.

In the 1830s, external forces combined to help Papineau and the *patriote* movement. The French population was becoming increasingly alarmed by the enormous influx of immigrants from the British Isles. The rich ones swelled the ranks of the detested merchants, and the poor Scots and Irish infested the cities and wandered the countryside. If immigration were allowed to continue at the present rate, the French might become outnumbered

This membership card of the Upper Canada Patriot Hunters shows the eagle (their symbol) swooping down on the lion (the symbol of Colonial government). After the uprisings of 1837 had failed, the Patriots organized themselves into secret chapters and planned new tactics for overthrowing the government.

in their own territory. It was the immigrant ships too, that had brought the cholera epidemic of 1832, an epidemic that had decimated the populations of Quebec City and of Montreal as well as those of rural areas. Although the *patriote* press had urged the closing of the ports, even though many immigrants were passing through to Upper Canada, the British merchants would not hear of it. Such a measure would be bad for trade. As a result of their obstinacy and of inadequate medical facilities, many thousands had died miserably and been hastily buried in the cholera cemeteries.

In addition to the cholera epidemics, the British were blamed for the poor economic conditions of the thirties. Years of insect plagues and alternating floods and droughts had ruined harvests. Habitants on their exhausted lands, especially in the countryside around Montreal, were destitute. It may have been silly to blame the British for the grasshoppers, but what the farmers actually saw were their gaunt and sickly families, living on a few peas and the carcasses of animals dead in the fields, while the British in the cities remained fat and their government seemed to do nothing. Many were forced to abandon the land. Some trekked south to Vermont; others clogged the cities, begging beside the immigrants.

rival urban mobs

By now there were factional newspapers and rival urban mobs like those in Upper Canada. Fiery speeches were being made, insults were being hurled, elections were bitter and rowdy. Young men from the Tory "Doric Club" roamed city streets, armed with axe-handles. But there was one difference: in addition to being divided along class lines, the factions were also divided by race. Although many of the poor Irish-Catholic immigrants sided with the French and the leaders of the *patriotes* included men with names like

O'Callaghan and Nelson, and although there were some rich Frenchmen who found it prudent and profitable to side with the colonial government, the bulk of the reformers tended to speak French and the Tories tended to be English-speaking.

the Ninety-Two Resolutions

The Tory merchants found it particularly infuriating that their opponents styled themselves "reformers." In their minds, *they* were the progressive, forward-looking element. It was they who wished to develop Lower Canada into a hive of commercial enterprise. The French, they felt, were backward, ignorant, tradition-bound and stagnant. There was some truth in this view. Papineau was far from being the equivalent of the hot-headed republican Mackenzie. He was, after all, a seigneur; a newly-created one, since his estate came into the family only with his father, but a seigneur nevertheless. If he had in fact come to power he would not have abolished class privileges or changed the seigneur-tenant system of the land ownership. The *patriotes*, unlike the Radicals of Upper Canada, talked reform in the service of an essentially conservative ethic.

Papineau was also more conservative than Mackenzie in his attitude towards armed rebellion. He had always won his battles through the normal political process. This was the method he wished to pursue, even after the British government had rejected the Ninety-Two Resolutions sent to it by the Assembly of Lower Canada, rejecting along with them the principle of responsible government for Lower Canada, and even after the governor had begun using tax money in flat disregard of the Assembly's authority and expressed wishes. At the mammoth meeting of the *patriotes* held at St Charles in October of 1837, a meeting complete with banners, flags and slogans, Papineau was almost the only *patriote* leader to speak for modera-

tion. But the lesser leaders seized control of the meeting and talked of sterner measures. They talked, in fact, of armed revolt, and the audience was with them.

Mackenzie plotted his revolt for months before it actually took place, but the *patriotes* were pushed into theirs before they were well prepared. After the St. Charles meeting the British seized the initiative. The governor, incensed by the jubilant reports of the meeting in the *patriote* press, issued warrants for the arrest of the leaders, including Papineau. The skirmishes that then took place between the British army and the *patriotes* were not viewed by the latter as rebellion, but as rightful resistance to illegal arrest.

The *patriotes* were superior in one thing only: force of numbers. But they were ill-equipped – on the average, only one in ten had a gun – and poorly trained and disciplined. Although many were crack shots, good at sniping from the woods, they were hunters, not soldiers, unused to the conditions of a pitched battle. And they were badly led. The politicians who had inspired them with words were not military strategists.

real bayonets, not scythes

The British soldiers, on the other hand, were professionals, and their guns, unlike those of the *patriotes*, were unlikely to run out of ammunition in the middle of a battle. Their cannons were made of iron, not wood. They had real bayonets, not scythes with shortened handles. And their families, if they had any, were far away, not waiting in nearby farmhouses, threatened and vulnerable.

The *patriotes* had one brief moment of triumph. They fought 350 British soliders to a standstill, barricaded in a stone house in the village of St. Denis. But the Church, always suspicious of any moves against authority, refused to bury their dead; supplies ran out, and other towns were not

**Robert Nelson
"Great Eagle"**

His secret society was called the Frères Chasseurs, but the members bore titles that sounded like parts in an amateur theatrical comedy of the period: Great Eagles, Eagles, Castors, Raquettes and Chasseurs. After the uprisings of 1837 had been snuffed, Robert Nelson, a Montreal doctor, and a handful of die-hards regrouped to plan new strategy for the liberation of the Canadas. New recruits to their "Hunters' Lodges" were initiated through an elaborate procedure of rituals, oaths, signals and passwords. It would all have been funny if Nelson hadn't been deadly serious. His plan was to march on Montreal, seize all banks, utilities and transportation lines, and confiscate property – all in the name of his provisional government. In February and November, 1838, he made two attempts to become "president of the new republic," but was forced back to the U.S., abandoned his glorious scheme, and went back to medicine.

The patriotes *of St. Denis repelled an attack by regulars and volunteers led by Colonel Gore. Confusion and poor roads frustrated Gore's plans for a surprise night attack: instead, his exhausted, half-frozen men met well-prepared defenders.*

A guard in the Queen's Volunteers stands sentry duty in Lower Canada, which became an armed camp after the last patriotes *were arrested.*

so well fortified. Morale sank, numbers of *patriotes* – and their leaders – vanished and the British were easily able to re-take St. Denis, and to take St. Charles, St. Benoit and St. Eustache as well. Many homes were sacked and burned, not by the army itself but by the volunteers – civilian Tories, Highlanders from Glengarry, Orangemen – who had joined them. Drunken and victorious, the volunteers smashed and looted, turning families out of their homes to freeze in the snow while the British commanders looked the other way. The French civilian population had spawned the *patriote* movement, so it had to be taught a lesson.

The lesson was well learned, though it was not the one the British had intended. They had tried to establish peace by repression. Instead, by 1838 the French population was even more opposed to them. The comparatively open and optimistic *patriotes* had become the secretive and bitter Frères Chasseurs, and a faith in the will of the people had been replaced by vengeful terrorism.

By this time Papineau was far away. He had never approved of armed resistance. He had watched from a distance while the British burned St. Denis. Now he was living in the United States, where he had fled under the name of Mr. Louis. Mackenzie was in the States too. After spending some time holed up miserably on Navy Island, in the Niagara River, with 150 men, proclaiming a provisional government and being shot at by 2,500 militia on the Canadian shore, he had been arrested by the Americans, ostensibly for violating the neutrality laws, but probably as a sop thrown by the Americans to the British government. His temporary imprisonment in Rochester, New York, moderated some of his admiration for American institutions, and, despite the help they promised for his cause, Mackenzie would have little to do with the Hunters. Similarly, Papineau washed his hands of the Frères Chasseurs. They were too re-

In the most serious encounter of the L.C. rebellion, soldiers defeated a patriote force at St. Eustache by burning the convent where they had barricaded themselves. The soldiers later looted the town and burned most of the buildings.

Nobody collected this reward for Papineau and, like other leaders of the rebellion, he regained respectability. A curious aspect of the rebellion is that most of those punished were the rank-and-file.

publican for him, and they did not follow due process. Papineau watched from the United States while England tried yet one more solution to the "Canadian problem."

The English solution was to appoint Lord Durham as governor general, for both Upper and Lower Canada. Someone with the nickname "Radical Jack" would at least be able to understand the rebels in both provinces, and the radical factions could hardly charge that the British had provocatively appointed an arch-Tory. Durham was well known as a reformer, and he proceeded to reform. He recommended the abolition of special political privilege and that Britain concede responsible government in the colonies. But although he was anathema to the Tories of Upper Canada and to those of Lower Canada as well, he failed to understand the emotions that had prompted the Lower Canadian uprisings. He arrived in Canada with his mind set against "the ab-

surd pretensions of race." Uniting Upper and Lower Canada, he felt, would give the British a majority in the elected Assembly, and nature would then take its course. The French, whom he saw as having no particular right to exist on a continent whose manifest destiny was obviously to become English-speaking, would be overwhelmed and assimilated and peace would prevail.

Few except the reformers of Upper Canada were pleased with Lord Durham. The British Government was not pleased, either. Durham had used extraordinary methods to dispose of the arrested leaders of the 1837 outbreak in Lower Canada. Instead of hanging them, as the Tories wished, thus creating instant martyrs to the French cause, or freeing them, as the French wished, he had sent eight of them into exile in the West Indies, after extracting confessions from them but without a trial. The British government overturned his decision, and Durham resigned and returned to Eng-

**Lord Durham
"Radical Jack"**

John Lambton was a thorn in the side of his family, Parliament and the British aristocracy. It made no sense for a man of his wealth and connections to champion reform. They nicknamed him "Radical Jack" and sent him packing on diplomatic missions to Russia. When violence erupted in the Colonies, Durham agreed to head the fact-finding commission. He arrived at Quebec in 1838, dismissed the Council, named a new, impartial governing body and set up an investigation into every aspect of the Colonies' affairs. He was instantly popular with reformers and moderates, French and English, alike. However, even radicals were stunned when, on Queen Victoria's coronation day, Radical Jack declared amnesty to the rebels. This was outrage! The decree was denied in London, and Durham resigned, leaving the completion of his *Report* to aides. Coincidentally, he returned home aboard a ship named the *Inconstant*.

land. Before his death in 1840, he completed his famous report, a milestone in the development of Canadian self-government and a monument to racial misunderstanding.

After Durham's departure, it was the turn of the Frères Chasseurs. Backed by money and supplies of arms, with cells throughout the province and with a well-conceived plan of action, they came nearer to succeeding. Unlike the earlier *patriotes* , they did not balk at the word *rebellion*. They seized the strategic seigneury of Beauharnois, twenty miles from Montreal, and awaited the arms that were to be acquired by a raid on the nearby Indian settlement of Caughnawaga.

wailing and lamentation

But their plan was defeated by an accident. An Indian woman looking for her runaway cow had seen the raiders coming and warned the men gathered in their church. The Indians, loyal to the British, ambushed and captured the raiders and turned them in. And Robert Nelson, the leader of the Frères Chasseurs, arriving from the States with money and more arms, was intercepted by alerted loyalist patrols. Again the uprising failed for want of arms, and again the army and the volunteers scoured the countryside. An eyewitness, Colonel Angus McDonell of the Glengarry Highlanders, wrote:

We proceeded towards Beauharnois by a forced march, burning and laying waste the country as we went along, and it was a most distressing and heart-rending scene to see this fine settlement so completely destroyed, the homes burned and laid in ashes, and I understand the whole country to St. Charles experienced the same fate. The wailing and lamentation of the women and children on beholding their homes in flames and their property destroyed, their husbands, fathers, sons and relations dragged along prisoners–

women perishing in the snow, and children frozen stiff by their side or scattered in black spots upon the snow–half-grown children running frantic in the woods, frightened at the sight of a friend or foe–and such of the inhabitants as did not appear, their houses were consigned to the flames, as they were supposed to be rebels.

This time, the arch-Tories had their way. There were to be no quick trips to the West Indies: the rebels were to hang. The arrested men were tried, not by judge and jury–the English on a jury would condemn outright, the French would acquit–but by court martial, for the country was now under martial law. Over twelve hundred had been jailed. Of these, 108 were tried, 98 were condemned, and, in the end, 12 were hanged. Fifty-eight were transported to Australia, and, after several months, the remainder were freed. By that time even the English were sick of the spectacle of public hangings, and the government did not wish to antagonize the still-hostile French yet further with more reprisals.

"rebels," traitors, Tories

The Tories in Upper Canada were influenced by no such considerations, and more men were hanged there than in Lower Canada. In Lower Canada, you could be arrested or have your house burnt simply for being French, but there was more sport to rebel-hunting in Upper Canada. The Tories there used the fear of an American invasion, inspired by the abortive Hunter attacks, to their own advantage. It allowed them to be even more rigorous in their pursuit and persecution of "rebels." Anyone who opposed them was in danger of being labelled a traitor. It was astonishing how many people were Tories now, who had never been Tories before. The improvised white cotton "badges" of the Radicals had of course disappeared–no one dared wear one–but the red

The Spirit of 1837

The spirit of 1837 was nothing like the fervour of the Sons of Liberty in America's War of Independence. Among the reformers, radicals, rebels, *patriotes*, or whatever one calls them, the mood was frustration. Even when the insurrection spilled into the streets, as at St. Eustache (below), the revolution was leaderless, disorganized and ill-timed.

The battle at St. Charles was a military mis-match. In a one-hour skirmish, Colonel Wetherall's regulars defeated a half-armed, untrained band of habitant patriotes.

"Rebellion"

The colonies were in the throes of a depression when the rebellions erupted. But the uprisings in both Upper and Lower Canada petered out without changing the politics and economy in either province. The response to radical grievances came from London, opening the way to self-government.

PROCLAMATION.

BY His Excellency SIR FRANCIS BOND HEAD,
Baronet, Lieutenant Governor of Upper Canada, &c. &c.

To the Queen's Faithful Subjects in Upper Canada.

In a time of profound peace, while every one was quietly following his occupations, feeling secure under the protection of our Laws, a band of Rebels, instigated by a few malignant and disloyal men, has had the wickedness and audacity to assemble with Arms, and to attack and Murder the Queen's Subjects on the Highway—to Burn and Destroy their Property—to Rob the Public Mails—and to threaten to Plunder the Banks—and to Fire the City of Toronto.

Brave and Loyal People of Upper Canada, we have been long suffering from the acts and endeavours of concealed Traitors, but this is the first time that Rebellion has dared to shew itself openly in the land, in the absence of invasion by any Foreign Enemy.

Let every man do his duty now, and it will be the last time that we or our children shall see our lives or properties endangered, or the Authority of our Gracious Queen insulted by such treacherous and ungrateful men. MILITIA-MEN OF UPPER CANADA, no Country has ever shewn a finer example of Loyalty and Spirit than YOU have given upon this sudden call of Duty. Young and old of all ranks, are flocking to the Standard of their Country. What has taken place will enable our Queen to know Her Friends from Her Enemies—a public enemy is never so dangerous as a concealed Traitor—and now my friends let us complete well what is begun—let us not return to our rest till Treason and Traitors are revealed to the light of day, and rendered harmless throughout the land.

Be vigilant, patient and active—leave punishment to the Laws—our first object is, to arrest and secure all those who have been guilty of Rebellion, Murder and Robbery.—And to aid us in this, a Reward is hereby offered of

One Thousand Pounds,

to any one who will apprehend, and deliver up to Justice, WILLIAM LYON MACKENZE ; and FIVE HUNDRED POUNDS to any one who will apprehend, and deliver up to Justice, DAVID GIBSON—or SAMUEL LOUNT—or JESSE LLOYD—or SILAS FLETCHER—and the same reward and a free pardon will be given to any of their accomplices who will render this public service, except he or they shall have committed, in his own person, the crime of Murder or Arson.

And all, but the Leaders above-named, who have been seduced to join in this unnatural Rebellion, are hereby called to return to their duty to their Sovereign—to obey the Laws—and to live henceforward as good and faithful Subjects—and they will find the Government of their Queen as indulgent as it is just.

GOD SAVE THE QUEEN.

Monday, 3 o'clock, P. M.
7th Dec.

☞ The Party of Rebels, under their Chief Leaders, is wholly dispersed, and flying before the Loyal Malitia. The only thing that remains to be done, is to find them, and arrest them.

Hundreds helped Mackenzie escape, even with this price on his head.

Daughter of one of the hostages at Beauharnois, Katherine Ellice painted her captors.

Van Dieman's Land

Captured rebels who were spared the noose were packed onto old, creaky ships and exiled to penal colonies in Bermuda, Australia or Van Dieman's Land (Tasmania). In the last, under the watchful eye of Lt.-Gov. John Franklin, the Arctic explorer (right), harsh treatment and heavy labour made their lives miserable. Life sentences strangled all hope of freedom until, in the 1840's, a campaign for their amnesty wrung pardons from the government.

Prisoners like Wait were allowed to pace the deck two and a half hours a day.

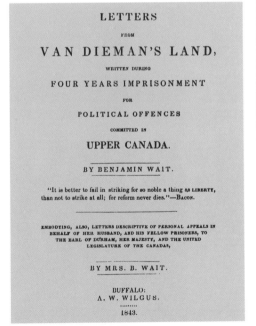

LETTERS

FROM

VAN DIEMAN'S LAND,

WRITTEN DURING

FOUR YEARS IMPRISONMENT

FOR

POLITICAL OFFENCES

COMMITTED IN

UPPER CANADA.

BY BENJAMIN WAIT.

"It is better to fail in striking for so noble a thing as LIBERTY, than not to strike at all; for reform never dies."—BACON.

EMBODYING, ALSO, LETTERS DESCRIPTIVE OF PERSONAL APPEALS IN BEHALF OF HER HUSBAND, AND HIS FELLOW PRISONERS, TO THE EARL OF DURHAM, HER MAJESTY, AND THE UNITED LEGISLATURE OF THE CANADAS,

BY MRS. B. WAIT.

BUFFALO:
A. W. WILGUS.
......
1843.

Before news of amnesty reached Van Dieman's Land, Benjamin Wait escaped to the U.S.A.

flannel ones of the Tories bloomed like the flowers of spring. Both the real Tories and the sham ones had a grand time breaking into homes on the pretence of looking for "rebels," roughing up women and children, stealing, burning, and settling old scores with their neighbours.

The treatment of one family during the search for Lount was typical. His nephew wrote, "After looting the place of all the light goods, such as socks, mittens, handkerchiefs, colars, shirts, and other similar things, and after partaking of a hearty meal of boiled pork, bread, cakes, pies, butter, preserves, and milk, they said they were quite satisfied Lount was not there." This raid was carried out by a party of thirty-five men, in the middle of the night. The terrified woman who opened the door at first thought they were Indians because they wore their coats pulled over their heads, and some of these boisterous groups did in fact dress like Indians painting their faces to disguise their identities and terrorize the victims.

hangings

In Upper Canada, a total of 885 men were arrested and thrown into jail. Ninety-two were transported, and twenty were hanged. The extreme Tories wanted the hangings to be a kind of loyalty circus, where people would turn out and cheer as the "rebels" took the drop. "The Tories," said one London commentator, "were big with hope that hanging rebels would be a very popular measure and expected five thousand spectators." But the hangings were virtually boycotted. This was not some alien invading force being hanged: these were neighbours, friends perhaps. The populace could not see the condemned men as vicious criminals, and the hangings sickened them. Many had been Mackenzie's sympathizers until he had taken up arms. They had rejected bloodshed and violence then, and they rejected it now.

Samuel Lount was arrested after days of near-escape. He hid for a while, then walked as far as Lake Erie. He and two others tried to row across the lake in a small boat. After two days, just as they were about to land on the American side, they were driven back by an adverse wind. A farmer mistook them for smugglers and turned them in. A petition urging Lount's pardon was signed by thousands of people, though Lount himself was pessimistic about the results. "Every name you get on that petition makes my death more sure," he said, and he was right. He was not killed by the will of the Upper Canadians, but by that of the new lieutenant-governor, Sir George Arthur, sent in by the British because of his reputation for ruthlessness. Before Canada, he'd been governor of the prison colony of Van Dieman's Land. He wanted to make an example of Lount.

"Mr. Jarvis, do your duty."

In April, 1838, Lount and Peter Matthews were hanged. John Ryerson wrote an account of the hanging to his brother Egerton:

At eight o'clock today, Thursday, the 12th, Lount and Matthews were executed. The gallows was erected just between the gaol and courthouse. Very few persons present, except the military and the ruf scruff of the city. The general feeling is in total opposition to the execution of these men. At their execution they manifested very good composure. Sheriff Jarvis burst into tears when he entered the room to prepare them for execution. They said to him very calmly, "Mr. Jarvis, do your duty. We are prepared to meet death and our Judge." They then, both of them, put their arms around his neck and kissed him. They were then prepared for the execution, they walked to the gallows with entire composure and

firmness of step. Mr. Richardson walked along side of Lount and Br. Beatty along side of Matthews. They ascended the scaffold and knelt down on the drop, the rope was fastened to their necks while they were on their knees. Mr. Richardson engaged in prayer & when he came to that part of the Lord's Prayer, "Forgive us our trespasses as we forgive them that trespass against us," the drop fell. My paper is full. I will write again next week. Ever yours,

J. Ryerson

political martyrs

But, as soon as they were dead, Lount and Matthews became political martyrs, an effect which the British had not anticipated and which may have prompted the cancellation of some further executions. Mackenzie himself, writing from Rochester, spoke for many when he headed an article on the hangings,

CANADA'S MARTYRS. – ROYAL MERCY!
ROB THE PEOPLE FIRST, THEN MURDER'EM
FOR DEFENDING THEMSELVES.

In the picture above the article, two men without faces swing from a gallows, and the windows of the jail are crowded with watchers. The jail was filled with men who could either hear or see the execution and who were expecting that they would shortly share their fate. To pass the time, many of them carved small objects out of wood. One prisoner made a small maple box, and on the bottom, where it would not at first be seen, he carved:

April 12th, 1838, alas for Lount and Matthews

This had to serve instead of a tombstone epitaph for Lount. Like all hanged men, he was buried in the Potter's Field.

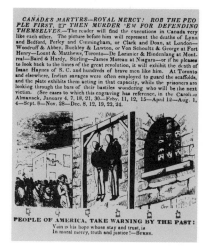

If you're looking for truth, justice or moral mercy you're wasting your time, the Caroline Almanack says. It condemns the hanging of Lount and Matthews, who were killed for their part in the Upper Canada rebellion.

King St., Toronto, 1835, shows an ox-cart stalled beside the Jail. The flagstone walk past St. James' Church was the promenade for fashionable society.

After the Ball

You think you can send me to the gallows, but I tell you that when you're frizzling with the devil, I'll be keeping tavern on Yonge Street.

John Montgomery, owner of Montgomery's Tavern

The tears of Sheriff William Jarvis at the hanging of Samuel Lount were quite genuine. Jarvis had led the picket responsible for routing the advance forces of Mackenzie, and he was thus inadvertently responsible for Lount's death. But he was also involved in the movement to stop the hanging. He hadn't forgotten that it was Lount who had kept Mackenzie from burning his home, where his wife and sick children were huddled during the radical advance. Mackenzie had already burned one Tory house and was heading for "Rosedale" when Lount said he wasn't there to fight women and sick children, and that if the men didn't stop, he would leave them. Apparently his word and his presence were both highly valued, for – against the wishes of Mackenzie – the advancing army turned aside. Meanwhile Mrs. Jarvis and the children, in a carriage full of blankets, had fled from the house and made their way to the harbour, where they took refuge on a steamboat.

Mary Jarvis, who had been Mary Powell until she married Sheriff Jarvis in 1827, had been a leading figure in upper class York society since her return from Jane English's New York finishing school. After her marriage, she had redecorated and expanded the Jarvis mansion, "Rosedale," which stood outside the city limits east of Yonge Street and Davenport Road. There she held court, both watching and participating in the enormous changes that had taken place in her town since the days when York was little more than a village.

Her finishing-school wardrobe would now have seemed quaint and immodest. Women's dresses had ballooned in the twenty-five years since the straight Empire silhouette had been the height of fashion. Now fashionable women resembled structures made of pumpkins: large bell-shaped skirts were nipped in tightly at the waist and topped with a long bodice, usually ending in a point below the waist, and two bulgy leg o'mutton sleeves, puffed above the elbow, close-fitting below it. Tight coats and *pelisses* were impossible over the new silhouette. Instead, women wore shawls and mantles. A cashmere shawl, sent by a relative in India if you happened to be lucky enough to have one, was considered the ultimate finishing touch. And out of sight but of equal importance, frilled, starched, boned and ruffled petticoats helped swell the skirts, while tightly-laced corsets pinched the waist. Underdrawers, too, had made their appearance. At first they were literally two separate drawers, one for each leg, tied at the waist by strings. Occasionally a string would come undone and the single drawer would drop embarrassingly to the floor. Silk was replacing muslin as the most desira-

Sons of Toronto's best families, who aspired to powdered wigs and courtrooms, were judged at Osgoode Hall by the Upper Canada Law Society: in 1837, one Robinson, one Strachan.

Muddy York

It was a treacherous, muddy place to tread. York (or Toronto, as it came
to be known in 1834) was still just a town: population 9,000; no waterworks;
no sewers; no paved roads; not even board sidewalks! It must have been an
unlikely place to settle. To most of the tourists, it was halfway between
Kingston (a civilized city) and that wonder of the world, Niagara Falls.

The lake and harbour: this is the Maitland wharf at Church Street.

This small structure of rough-hewn timber was York's first post office.

Joseph Bloor supplied his Farmer's Arms Inn with ale from his brewery in York.

York's harbour greeted flatbottoms, canoes, tall ships and paddle wheelers.

ble fabric, and no lady was complete without a tiny silk parasol, which, with the aid of the deep-brimmed bonnets, prevented her nose from sprouting those stigmata of the outdoor working classes, freckles. A servant or a farmer's wife had one consolation: she was not obliged to be fashionable and could thus be much more comfortable. The tight waists and ungainly skirts of the upper classes served the same function for their women as bound feet did for the Chinese.

Even more dramatic changes had taken place in Mary's city. The village of under a thousand was now over fifteen times its former size, and had been incorporated in 1834 under its new name, Toronto. As befitted a real city, street names were now posted and houses were numbered. Street lighting – by that new wonder fuel, gas – was being planned. Instead of the earlier jumble of living and building styles, Toronto now had districts. Urban conditions spawned slums, and Toronto's were east of Yonge Street, around the market. This area, naturally, had a high concentration of inns, taverns and gin shops. The red light district, where prostitutes more urbane than those of the more northern small-town or logging-camp "she-bang" strolled the streets or worked more comfortably in "houses of ill fame," was on Lombard Street. The rich lived on Front Street overlooking the bay, or, like Mary Jarvis, on suburban estates.

scarlet uniforms and moustaches

Toronto, like the York of old and like most colonial cities, still had a garrison, but its inhabitants and activities were no longer the only social focus of the town. The garrison itself, some thought, was looking a little tatty. Since there hadn't been a real war for almost twenty-five years (right-thinking officers didn't count that paltry Mackenzie business) it was hard for officers to bask in the light of recent exploits. Still, scarlet uniforms and mous-

taches made a fine show on the dance floor, and young soldiers were more impressive to the local belles than were young businessmen, who had no facial ornaments but mutton-chop whiskers. Almost every city had its "Tandem Club" to which young officers of the garrison belonged. The clubs held sleighing outings every week during the winter months. In Toronto, they started from Osgoode Hall and usually went along King Street and from there to some country inn, where they would have a bucolic feast with lots to drink, before returning. Each officer would have a respectable young lady tucked beside him under the furs. These girls were referred to as "muffins," presumably because they were warm and, in the winter costume of the day, round in shape.

the strange new breed of man

The houses at which the officers collected their "muffins" were likely to be brick instead of wood. To have a brick house was now a status symbol; and brick, its admirers urged, was less flammable. House fires were still a hazard, but Toronto now had a fire hall, and the volunteer fireman system was coming in. It also had a hospital, though, considering the lack of antiseptics and the ignorance of disease, this was no great improvement. Women in childbed were much better off at home, since physicians in hospitals had a habit of attending them right after the dissection of a corpse, without washing their hands. Even the age of the factory was starting to reach Toronto, for in addition to the earlier gristmills and distilleries, there were now an axe factory, a soap factory and a paper factory. Small houses had been built in "Macaulay Town," north of Queen and Yonge, to accommodate the strange new breed of man who worked in them. Not a servant, farm labourer, craftsman, or tradesman, he was already beginning to develop into a distinct species. In future this urban work-

Jesse Ketchum
Tanner of Yonge St.

Among the earliest settlers in York was a quiet and generous man named Jesse Ketchum. In 1799, at age 17, he arrived from Buffalo, N.Y., to take charge of his brother's tanning business at the corner of Newgate (Adelaide) and Yonge. The Ketchum landholdings in "Little York" were considerable, extending north from King to Queen and west from Yonge to Bay Street. But Ketchum was a liberal man, in both his views and donations, and he gave of his land and money as he saw the need. He was a supporter of free education and in 1828 collided with John Strachan over common schools. He was the first to build sidewalks (of tan bark) in the muddy town and contributed £325 in 1822 to have a bridge built across the Don River. He was active in temperance groups and donated several acres of land in Yorkville for a children's park.

Staunch defender of Tory and Anglican privilege, outspoken critic of anything that smacked of reform, John Strachan, shown here in old age, was Toronto's first bishop and university founder.

ing class would more than once make life unpleasant for the town's rich and powerful.

"Fancy Dress Ball"

But this distant threat, and the recent uprisings which had menaced them in a much more direct way, did not keep the rulers from celebrating their triumph. Despite her distress over the impending fate of Lount, Mary Jarvis threw a "Fancy Dress Ball" for four hundred people at the end of the 1837-38 winter season. For this occasion, Rosedale was decorated from end to end. It was heated by extra stoves, lighted by the new coal-oil lamps with coloured glass shades, and festooned with flowers. The verandah was enclosed and fitted up as a picture gallery, where guests tired of dancing could stroll. Mary Jarvis dressed herself as "Mrs. Leo Hunter," a character out of Dickens's "Pickwick Papers," for Charles Dickens had replaced Walter Scott as the literary hero of the day. Soon the virtues of respectable middle-class family life would eclipse the glories of romantic outlawry and the wild picturesque. But many of the costumes were reminiscent of the Marquis of Tweedale's Ball back in 1815. The upper class still found it amusing to dress up as Indians and poor people, though it was now funny to impersonate black Americans and Chinese as well. While the costumes were similar, the dancers were probably less smelly than those of that earlier era. Washing all over, which had once been thought of as dangerous to the health, was becoming accepted, and the very best houses, such as Allan MacNab's "Dundurn" on Hamilton Mountain, had "ablution rooms" in them where one could immerse oneself in hot water in a container very much like a modern bathtub. Cleanliness, if not yet seen as next to godliness, was beginning to be both possible and desirable.

One masquerade guest came as "Hans Van

Slapperbottom, the Canadian Patriot General (a most unvarnished loafer)," intended as a joke at the expense of Colonel Van Egmond, the gallant old cavalry officer who had tried, too late and in vain, to forge Mackenzie's undisciplined men into a successful military force. Thus, while trials and reprisals went on all over the province, the fashionables of Toronto society laughed at the uprisings and danced their cares away.

But there was an ominous cloud on their horizon. A newspaper wit, writing in *The Colonist* of 1839, turned the laugh on the dancers in a burlesque drama.

MESSENGER:

Oh the dreadful news!
That both the Canadas in one be joined – (faints).

SHERIFF WILLIAM:

Farewell, ye masquerades, ye sparkling routs:
Now routed out, no more shall routs be ours...
... No: this news that slays our warmest hopes,
Ends pageantry, and pride and masquerade.

The prophecy proved true. The battle of Yonge Street may not have been large, but the aftereffects were both wide-ranging and long-lasting. It was obvious that the Radicals had lost. But, strangely enough, the Tories lost as well. The measures recommended by "Radical Jack" Durham and implemented in the forties, including the union of the two Canadas and the extension of power to the "Liberal," "Moderate" or "Reform" parties, deprived the Family Compact and their allies of the stranglehold on the province they had fought so long to maintain.

* * *

The uprisings in Upper and Lower Canada were not the only things that happened in 1837. In that year Victoria ascended the throne of England and Joe Howe entered the legislature of Nova Sco-

tia. Nova Scotians long regarded the latter event as at least of equal importance with the former.

Like Mary Jarvis's York, Joe Howe's Halifax had been through many changes since the heady days right after the end of the War of 1812. Peace meant, of course, a reduction in the garrison, and many of the British officers moved back to England, leaving their fine homes empty. There were no more privateers and no more rich prizes to be auctioned in Halifax Harbour. Farmers could no longer get the high prices they'd been able to demand when their produce was used for provisioning the army and navy; in addition, they were hit by several years of bad weather and crop failure. The West Indies trade was affected by competition with the United States, and the freeing of the slaves there meant higher prices for rum. And immigrants even poorer than the poorest of the inhabitants began to flow into the province. Nova Scotia usually got the worst of the shiploads, since it was the colony closest to Britain and the most unscrupulous of the shippers used it as a dumping ground. The immigrants brought cholera, and Halifax, like every other colonial city, had an epidemic of it in the early thirties. The capitalists of the city took their money out of circulation, which was why, when Joe Howe went subscription-collecting in the twenties for his newspaper *The Novascotian*, he found many men with good houses but no actual cash.

public opinion

Newspapers, too, had changed since 1815, and Joe Howe had helped to change them. He went into debt to buy *The Novascotian*, and at first he not only printed the paper but, with the help of his wife, wrote most of it as well. The early papers were glorified notice-boards, but Howe bent his paper to more sophisticated purposes, using it to both mould and reflect public opinion. When he

KINGSTON RACES.
September Meeting, 1839.

THE Kingston Races are fixed to take place on Tuesday and Wednesday, 24th and 25th September.

PATRONS,
Col. the Hon. H. Dundas, C. B., Commodore Sandom, R. N.

PRESIDENT,
John B. Marks, Esq.

VICE PRESIDENT,
James Sampson, Esq.

STEWARDS.
The Sheriff,   Col. Hill, 4th Batt.
The Mayor,   Capt. Otway, R. A.
J. S. Cartwright, Esq. Lieut. Fowell, R. N.
T. Kirkpatrick, Esq. Capt. Stubbman, 83rd.
J. R. Forsyth, Esq. Lieut. Barry, 65th.
Thomas Greer, Esq. Lieut. St. Aubyn, 83d.
W. R. Sanders, Esq. Lieut. Harrison, R. A.
  Henry Smith, Esq. Treasurer, T. A.
Corbett, Esq. Clerk of the Course.
Further particulars will be published in due time.
            JOHN ROY, Secretary.
Kingston, 8th July, 1839.   3z

Oh, the Kingston racetrack's five miles long ... and the ad tells racing fans that the races are fixed—to take place, that is, in two months.

On the evening of January 14, 1837, fire ignited on Peter's Wharf and swept through the market of Saint John, N.B., destroying most of the old city. The glow was seen in Fredericton, 90 miles away.

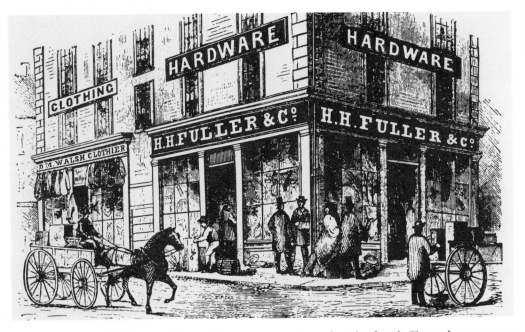

Market Square in Halifax was busy with commerce at the end of the decade. Horse-drawn wagons and pushcarts rattled past H. H. Fuller's hardware store, making their pick-up and delivery rounds.

finally moved against the oligarchy who controlled the province through the "Council of Twelve" without reference to the people or to their elected representatives, it was his newspaper he used to strike the first blow. In it he accused the Halifax magistrates of incompetence and corruption. They sued him for libel, and though he was told he had no case in law, he undertook his own defence, spoke eloquently for six hours straight, and was acquitted. He was carried home in triumph on the shoulders of the crowd, who saw his victory as their own and promptly elected him to the legislature. He was only thirty-two.

a sordid printer

Howe must have read of the events in the Canadas with concern as well as with that wry irony with which Maritimers habitually view any doings much west of Fredericton. The failure of Mackenzie and Papineau was going to make it much harder for him to implement change without getting himself hanged. In fact, the struggle for "Responsible Government" – real self-government for British North Americans – was to take ten years of savage verbal and political infighting. Howe himself was challenged to duels and attacked by mobs. Attempts were made to smash his press. His personal life was slandered and he was cursed by the Tories as an upstart and a vulgarian, a sordid printer. Tory wives and daughters "cut" him on the street. As Howe himself said, "They have scorned me at their feasts, and they have insulted me at their funerals." (Funerals at that time were major social events.) But, in the end, friendships were broken, but no heads; characters were assassinated, but no politicians. Perhaps Howe fared better than Mackenzie because of his reliance on persuasion rather than force of arms, perhaps because the opposition was less bloodthirsty. But also he was arguing from an essentially British

120

The Adventures of Sam Slick

Now Sam Slick, he knew the lay of the land, and its people too. "What a pity it is marryin' spoils courtin'," he quipped in his usual cracker-barrel style. Sam didn't have much use for book-wisdom neither: "Books only weaken understandin', as water does brandy." Sam Slick of Slickville was the fictional creation of Thomas Chandler Haliburton, and made his first appearance in 1835. Though his author has been dubbed "the father of American humour," Sam's wit is true "Bluenose."

Thomas Chandler Haliburton, born in Windsor, N.S., in 1796, was a lawyer and judge before retiring to English politics in 1841.

Sam Slick of Slickville, fictional character and outlet for the wit and wisdom of Judge Haliburton, first appeared in 1835, poking fun at life's little problems.

This advertisement shows how reliant the Maritimes, and most of Canada, were on American and British goods.

Tory position: he didn't want anything more for Nova Scotians than the rights an Englishman took for granted.

In 1840, the battle had just begun. But Howe had more than political wrangling to think about. Transportation, for instance. He had first-hand experience of the badness of the roads, so it wasn't surprising that the idea of a Nova Scotian railroad should have appealed to him. Railroads had already spread across the United States, from twenty-three miles of rail in 1830 to twenty-eight hundred by 1840. Canada's first railway using a moving steam engine, the Champlain and St. Lawrence Railway, was opened in 1836. Its little engine pulled two open cars and took thirty minutes to go fifteen miles, but this was incomparably faster and more comfortable that the bumpy stagecoaches. The Erie and Ontario used horse-drawn carriages. Despite these primitive beginnings, Howe could see great possibilities for railroads, and was advocating them as early as 1835.

He was enthusiastic, too, over another use of steam. In 1838, after his election, Howe sailed to England with his good friend T. C. Haliburton. Haliburton, who had first been published by Howe, had made a literary hit in England with his "Sam Slick" sketches, and the two, flushed with their respective victories, were off to tour Europe. As their sailing ship lay becalmed several hundred miles from England, they were overtaken by a new breed of ship, the steamship *Sirius*. Howe went on board to drink a glass of champagne with the captain, and was so impressed with the ship's style, grace and speed that he and Haliburton lobbied the British Colonial Office as soon as they hit England. Wouldn't a fleet of steamers be better for carrying the mail than the old tubs they were using? For once the government moved quickly, and by 1840 Samuel Cunard, another Haligonian, had formed his steamship company and was ferrying the Royal Mail. Nova Scotia was now only fourteen days away from England instead of fifty. Strangely enough, Howe did not see the threat posed to Nova Scotia's now flourishing shipbuilding industry by the combination of steamships and the new steam railways.

But in 1840, that threat was far in the future. Cheering crowds jammed Halifax Harbour to greet the arrival of the first Cunard ship, which seemed to be another triumph for Nova Scotia shipbuilders. In fact, the whole shore was now a shipyard, and the province turned out one fast clipper ship after another. Some they sold, some they used to carry on their own vigorous trade, in timber, tea, fish, even ice – anything that would float and sell. Nova Scotia was prosperous again and Joe Howe was there to inspire and lead it. What could go wrong?

The so-called gentry of Montreal adopted the airs and habits of British aristocracy. In this engraving titled "A Real Scene in Montreal," farmers and servants take a dim view of the portly fox hunters who have trespassed their land and flattened their crops.

Acknowledgements

It would not have been possible for me to work on this book without the help of my research assistant, Carolyn Moulton, who combed through libraries in Toronto in search of period documents while I awaited the results sixty miles north, snowbound and housebound with a new baby. She found the Baldwin Room and the Central Reference Library especially helpful. I read many recent books on my subjects, a number of which were supplied by my father, C.E. Atwood. My two aunts, Joyce Barkhouse and Kay Cogswell, generously lent me the Nova Scotian materials they had collected for several related projects. I must mention, too, the helpful nagging of Michael Bliss, especially in connection with Quebec material.

I should also acknowledge my house, which was built in the 1840s and was probably a "second house," the dream home that succeeded the log shanty of the first settlement period. It has a front parlour with window-mouldings noticeably thicker than those of the inferior back parlour, and now that I know more about its probable inhabitants I view the impressiveness, the luxury even, of those window-mouldings with new respect. The piles of rocks in the fields behind the house have taken on fresh significance as well; I now know how many hours of back-breaking if not heart-breaking labour must have gone into hauling those rocks. My house is still known by the name of the family who originally settled the land—though no one of that name has lived in it for decades—but that seems only fitting.

Margaret Atwood

Photo: Graeme Gibson

The Author

Margaret Atwood was born in Ottawa in 1939 and grew up in that city, in Sault Ste. Marie and in Toronto, spending every spring, summer, and fall in the northern Quebec or Ontario bushland with her family. In 1961 after graduating from Victoria College, University of Toronto, where she was writer-in-residence little more than a decade later, she took her A.M. at Radcliffe College, Harvard. Her first poetry collection, *The Circle Game*, won the Governor General's Award in 1966. Since then, she has published five books of poetry, the critical survey of Canadian literature, *Survival,* three novels, most recently, *Lady Oracle*, and a collection of short stories, *Dancing Girls.*

Index

The page numbers in italics refer to illustrations and captions

Picture Credits

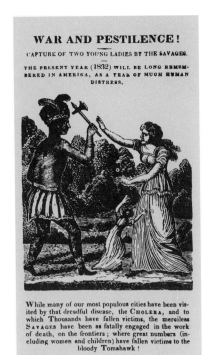

There was indeed war and pestilence on the land in the days of the rebels. Dissent, disease, a severe depression and distrust of the colonial leaders marked the period. What the next decade would bring, nobody knew.

We would like to acknowledge the help and co-operation of the directors and staff of the various public institutions and the private firms and individuals who made available paintings, posters, mementoes, collections and albums as well as photographs and gave us permission to reproduce them. Every effort has been made to identify and credit appropriately the sources of all illustrations used in this book. Any further information will be appreciated and acknowledged in subsequent editions.

The illustrations are listed in the order of their appearance on the page, left to right, top to bottom. Principal sources are credited under these abbreviations:

P A C   Public Archives of Canada
M T C L Metropolitan Toronto Central Library
R O M   Royal Ontario Museum
O C   Osbourne Collection of Early Children's Books
         Metropolitan Toronto Central Library
A N Q   Archives Nationales du Québec
D U L   Dalhousie University Library, Halifax, N.S.

/1 MTCL /2 PAC /4 The Wellcome Museum, London, England /6 DUL /7 OC /8 MTCL /9 New Brunswick Museum - Archives Section /10 PAC /11 private collection /12 PAC /13 Molson's Archives /14 Château de Ramezay, Montreal /15 *Canadian Book of Printing*, MTCL /16,17 Château de Ramezay, Montreal; private collections /18,19 PAC /20 Legislative Library, Province House, Halifax, N.S. /21 Molson's Archives /22 PAC /23 Sigmund Samuel Library; PAC /24 National Gallery of Canada, Ottawa /25 PAC /26 *Illustrated London News*; private collection /27 *Illustrated London News* /28 Ryerson Press Archives /29 Archives de Monastère du L'hôtel-Dieu de Québec; Montreal General Hospital; MTCL; Montreal General Hospital; Archives de Monastère du L'hôtel-Dieu de Québec; private collection /30 OC; MTCL /31 DUL /32 ROM; private collection /33 PAC /34 MTCL /35 Webster Canadiana Collection, The New Brunswick Museum /36 Montreal Museum of Fine Arts /37 OC /38 Inventaire des Biens Culturels du Québec /39 PAC /40 Public Archives of P.E.I. /41 PAC /42 private collection /43 MTCL /44 *Mrs. Porter's Cook Book* /45 University of Toronto Library; University of Toronto Press; PAC; MTCL, Fine Arts Collection /46 MTCL /47 MTCL; MTCL; MTCL; MTCL; National Library of Canada; private collection /48,49 PAC /50 ROM /51 PAC /52 Winnipeg *Tribune*; PAC /53 MTCL; PAC /54 private collection /55 Manitoba Archives; PAC /56 Office du film de la Province de Québec /57 McCord Museum, Montreal /58 PAC /59,60, 61,62 MTCL /63 PAC /64 private collection /65 Public Archives of Nova Scotia /66 McCord Museum, Montreal /67 National Gallery of Canada, Ottawa /68 Abby Aldrich Rockefeller Folk Art Collection /69 PAC /70 ANQ; MTCL /71 PAC /72 private collection /73 MTCL; MTCL; private collection /74 Quebec Literary and Historical Society /75 MTCL; Canadian National /76 PAC; ROM /77 McCord Museum; MTCL /78 National Gallery of Canada, Ottawa /79 Webster Canadiana Collection, The New Brunswick Museum /80 ROM /81 National Library of Canada /82 ANQ /83 MTCL; PAC /84 New Brunswick Museum /85 Dundurn Castle, Hamilton /86 MTCL, Fine Arts Picture Collection /87 PAC /88 MTCL /89 PAC; PAC; Jewish Public Library, Montreal; MTCL /90 National Gallery of Canada, Ottawa /92 PAC /93,94 MTCL /95 PAC /96 ANQ /97,98 MTCL /99,100 PAC /101 MTCL; /101 ANQ /103 ANQ; *Folk Songs of Canada*, Edith Fowke /104 PAC /105 ANQ /106 MTCL, John Ross Robertson Collection; PAC /107 PAC; ANQ /108 MTCL /109, 110 MTCL, John Ross Robertson Collection /111 private collection; PAC /112 PAC; National Library of Canada /113 MTCL /114 PAC /115 private collection /116 ROM; MTCL; ROM; Webster Canadiana Collection, The New Brunswick Museum /117,118 MTCL /119 private collection /120 New Brunswick Museum /121 DUL; MTCL, Fine Arts Picture Collection; Special Collections, DUL /122 DUL /123 PAC /128 National Library of Canada.

1829

Egerton Ryerson establishes the *Christian Guardian* in Toronto.

Thomas Chandler Haliburton's *Historical and Statistical Account of Nova Scotia,* is published.

John Beverley Robinson appointed chief justice of U.C.

300-mile roadway completed from Detroit River to York, U.C. under administration of Col. Thomas Talbot.

1830

John Galt publishes *Lawrie Todd.*

Brandy Dispute pits N.S. liquor interests against government.

1831

British explorer James Clark Ross locates the North Magnetic Pole.

Lower Fort Garry is built.

William Lyon Mackenzie expelled from the assembly of U.C. for libel.

1832

William "Tyger" Dunlop publishes *Statistical Sketches of Upper Canada.*

Immigration reaches peak as 66,000 arrive to settle in Upper Canada.

EMIGRATION.

THE

ADVANTAGES

OF

EMIGRATION TO CANADA,

BEING THE SUBSTANCE OF

Two Lectures,

DELIVERED AT THE

TOWN-HALL, COLCHESTER,

AND THE

MECHANICS' INSTITUTION, IPSWICH,

BY

WILLIAM CATTERMOLE.

May, 1831.

LONDON:

SIMPKIN AND MARSHALL; THE BOOKSELLERS AT IPSWICH AND COLCHESTER; J. LODER, WOODBRIDGE.

W. L. Mackenzie visits England with petitions for the redress of grievances in Upper Canada.

Cholera epidemic in B.N.A. kills thousands.

CHOLERA BULLETIN.

Printed at the Wesleyan Office.

TO the President of the Board of Health of the Gore District:

Sir----I have this morning received a communication from Doct. GILPIN of Brantford, stating he was called to visit Three cases, which he considers exhibited characters of Spasmodic Cholera. One case, a man by the name of Young, proved fatal in 8 hours. The other two were convalescent when Doctor Gilpin writes.

The following is a report I submit to the Board of Health, on the above cases:

Cases of CHOLERA in the Gore District, from June 23, to June 26, inclusive----

Brantford, Cases THREE, Deaths 1, Convalescent 2.

(Signed)   SLADE ROBINSON,
         Pres't Medical Board.

Hamilton, June 27, 1832.

Major John Richardson publishes *Wacousta.*

The Rideau Canal between Bytown and Kingston completed.

Representative government granted to the colony of Nfld.

Newfoundland's *St. John's Times* founded.

1833

The British American Land Company acquires 800,000 acres of land for sale in Eastern Townships, L.C.

John Molson's *Royal William* is first steamship to cross the Atlantic.

Captain George Back makes overland journey to the Arctic Ocean.

Father Belcourt establishes an Indian mission on the Assiniboine.

Welland Canal completed between Lake Ontario and Lake Erie.

Montreal Daily Advertiser — first daily in Canada.

1834

York renamed Toronto.